The Essential Guide to Musical Theatre for

THE
SHOW MUSICIAN

BROADWAY · TOURING · WEST END

ÁGÚST SVEINSSON

Copyright © 2017 Ágúst Sveinsson

Cover Design © 2017 by Ágúst Sveinsson

All rights reserved. No part of this publication may be reproduced, distributed, or transmitted in any form or by any means, including photocopying, recording, or other electronic or mechanical methods, without the prior written permission of the publisher, except in the case of brief quotations embodied in critical reviews and certain other non-commercial uses permitted by copyright law.

ISBN: 1530866243

ISBN-13: 978-1530866243

This book is dedicated to my wife, Monique, and my daughters, Isabelle and Sienna. You are my world.

IV

Acknowledgements

I would like to thank my editor, Allister Thompson, for his expert editing and invaluable input. Thanks to all my friends and colleagues who helped in so many ways in the creation of this book. Many thanks to my brother and my parents for all your love and support. To my wife and my daughters, thank you for all your love, support, and patience.

All your help and input has been invaluable. Thank you all so much.

VI

Table of Contents

ABOUT THE AUTHOR	1
INTRODUCTION	3
1 - THE SKILLS NEEDED TO SUCCEED	7
Personal Skills	7
Musical Skills	11
2 - HOW TO GET WORK IN MUSICAL THEATRE	29
Get Out There!	30
Networking	30
Self-Promotion	31
London - New York	36
Education	39
Fixers (UK)/Musical Contractors (US)	40
Musical Supervisor	43
Musical Director (MD)/Conductor	44
Your Reputation	44
Amateur Theatre	45
Cruise Ships	45
Pantomimes	46

The Dep/The Sub	50
Perseverance!	51
3 - THE BIG BREAK	**53**
Depping/Subbing	53
The NA: The Never Again	60
How Do You Become the Regular Player on a Show?	61
4 - WORKING IN MUSICAL THEATRE	**64**
The Different Types of Shows in Musical Theatre	69
Definition of a West End and a Broadway Theatre	71
Show Performance Times	72
What Can I Expect to Get Paid?	74
UK Touring Shows	87
US Touring Shows	88
Other Relevant Information	90
Taking Time Off	94
The EPK: Electronic Press Kit	104
The Show Report	106
5 - WORKING IN A PIT ENVIRONMENT	**107**
The Pit Setup	108
Common Pit Equipment	117

Pit Monitoring	121
Pit Etiquette	124
Pit Attire	127
Setting Up and Packing Up	129
6 - WHO'S WHO IN THEATRE	**130**
The Creative Team	131
Personnel Working Directly With the Show	132
On-Site Creative Team	134
Technical Team	135
The Music Team	136
In-House Personnel	136
Onstage Team	137
7 - THE MUSICAL DIRECTOR (MD)/CONDUCTOR	**139**
The Musical Director/Conductor	139
The Assistant MD/Associate Conductor	140
The Types of MD	141
Following an MD	142
Being an MD/Conductor	144
8 - A WEEK IN THE LIFE OF A SHOW MUSICIAN	**148**
A Week in the Life of a West End Musician	149

A Week in the Life of a UK Touring Musician	152
The Tech Week/Production Period	159

9 - EQUIPMENT — 165

Keyboards	165
Guitars	166
Drums	167
Percussion	169
Front Line, Strings, and Specialist Instruments	169
Equipment Maintenance	169
Instrument Endorsement Deals	171

10 - THE UNIONS — 173

The Musicians' Union — UK	174
The American Federation of Musicians — USA	176
Other Union Benefits	178
Union Websites	179

11 - TOURING — 180

The Touring Process	181
The Get-In	183
The Sound Check	184
The UKT Agreement (UK Touring)	186

Travel	187
Parking	190
Subsistence	192
Digs	194
Accommodation Online Booking Tools	202
Foreign/International Venues	203
Organisation	205
Staying Fit and Healthy	206
Touring in the United States	207
12 - HOW A SHOW IS PUT TOGETHER	**210**
13 - BEING SELF-EMPLOYED	**216**
Time Management	216
Tax and Money Management	218
Expenses	219
Do I Need an Accountant?	224
Organising Your Accounts	226
Saving For Tax	227
UK National Insurance	228
Registering as Self-Employed	229
Sole Trader	229

Limited Company	230
VAT	231
Accounting Software	232
Useful Tax Resources	234
14 - OTHER USEFUL INFORMATION	**235**
Musicians' Union in the UK (MU)	235
American Federation of Musicians (AFM)	236
Other Useful Websites and Resources	237
Essential Listening	238
CLOSING	**240**
APPENDIX - GLOSSARY OF TERMS USED IN THEATRE	**241**

About the Author

Ágúst Sveinsson was born in Reykjavik, Iceland, and has worked as a professional drummer for over twenty-five years. In that time he has covered most styles of music, including pop, rock, funk, jazz, big band, Latin, and everything in between. He has worked in musical theatre for twenty years and has played on some of the biggest and most popular productions in the world, including performing in the West End of London as well as touring the world. Ágúst's experience and versatility has kept him busy in the very competitive business of musical theatre, and his repertoire of shows is ever increasing.

Musicals that Ágúst has worked on include: *Fame, Jesus Christ Superstar, Summer Holiday, Tell Me on a Sunday, Joseph and the Amazing Technicolor Dreamcoat, Grease, Footloose, The Wedding Singer, Rent, High School Musical, Hairspray, Sister Act, High School Musical 2, 9 to 5 the Musical, Priscilla Queen of the Desert, Godspell, Little Shop of Horrors*, and more.

In his many years as a professional drummer, Ágúst has shared the stage with bands such as The Spice Girls, The Sugarcubes (with Björk), and Let Loose, and he has worked with numerous bands and some of the biggest artists in musical theatre and the pop world, including Dave Finnegan (The Commitments), Darren Day, Suzanne Shaw (Heresay), Christopher Biggins, Glen Carter, Patsy Palmer (*EastEnders*), Faye Tozer (Steps), Marty Webb, Bryan Conley, Maureen Nolan (The Nolan Sisters), Ben Richards, Natalie Casey, Jonathan Wilkes, Letitia Dean (*EastEnders*), Noel Sullivan (Heresay), The Chuckle Brothers, Michael Ball, Micky Dolenz

About the Author

(The Monkees), The Krankies, Les Dennis, Mickey Starke, John Barrowman, Bonnie Langford, Cynthia Erivo, Duncan James (Blue), and Jason Donovan.

Ágúst is a highly trained musician. At an early age he studied music at FIH, the most renowned jazz college in Iceland. There he studied with Reynir Sigurðsson, the principal percussionist at the Icelandic Symphony Orchestra, considered one of Iceland's best percussion teachers. After moving to the UK, he was accepted into the Lancashire County Big Band, an early training ground for some of the UK's top musicians. While finishing his A-level music studies, Ágúst received a grant to study with one of UK's most renowned drum teachers, Dave Hassell, with whom he studied for over five years. Ágúst was then accepted into the highly sought-after music course at Salford University in Manchester. There in his first year of studies he auditioned for and was accepted into the award-winning University Big Band. Ágúst graduated from university with a Bachelor of Arts honours degree in music and sound recording.

Ágúst now lives with his family in Cambridgeshire, where he runs his drum studio and teaching practice, alongside his busy playing schedule. His teaching experience spans over twenty years, and his proven teaching methods get his students ready for the real world of the professional drummer in a very practical and constructive way, as well as emphasizing the importance of having fun.

For more information, please visit www.agustsveinsson.com and www.showmusician.com

Introduction

The last twenty years have seen — and continue to see — considerable changes in the music industry. Arguably, these changes have affected musicians within the business more than most. Where musicians find paid work is changing, and it is becoming increasingly difficult to find enough work to make a living. The world of the session musician is more or less gone, and players have to adapt to earn a decent wage. Yet there are many avenues that a musician can take, such as teaching or doing home recording sessions, to name just two. However, if you want to keep playing your instrument and working with other musicians, many are turning to musical theatre. It is one of the few ways a musician can earn a regular and decent living from playing in today's changing music scene.

The modern Western musical is still gaining popularity around the world and is ever-evolving, with adaptations of Hollywood movies and popular music drawing in new and younger audiences across the world. The two best-known places for musicals are without a doubt the West End of London and Broadway in New York City. Furthermore, productions can now be found in every major city and range from big blockbuster musicals such as *Wicked*, *Les Misérables,* and *Mamma Mia*, to small amateur shows and everything in between. Some are resident in a town or city, while many will travel from place to place. There is now a touring circuit in most Western countries, with numerous productions travelling year-round, and some even touring the world, so if you're serious about becoming a professional

Introduction

musician, there's every chance that you will play a musical theatre production at some point in your career. However, the size of bands in musical theatre is decreasing, and the days of twenty-piece pit orchestras are pretty much gone. It is now common to have just six or seven musicians on a musical, and even as few as three. Subsequently, the jobs are few and sought-after, making the industry highly competitive.

When I got my first job on a musical, I was amazed at how different an experience it was to what I was used to. Up to that point, most of my live playing experiences were based around playing with a band on stage to a dance floor full of people. I quickly discovered that there were so many other elements involved in my performance when playing a show that I had never previously experienced, been taught before, or even told about. Although I had completed a degree in music, not once had I been informed about all the different skills I needed to learn and develop if I wanted to work in musical theatre. There were numerous things I just didn't know, both musically and about the musical theatre scene as a whole. This included things like working in a pit environment, depping ('subbing' in the United States), and who a fixer or musical contractor was, just to name a few. Then there were the more practical aspects, such as booking digs (accommodation) on tour, how to deal with tax, and many other matters. Having worked in musical theatre for a long time, I believe that developing an understanding of how a theatre production works, the working environment, and the theatre industry is invaluable in making you a more adaptable and professional musician. Possessing this knowledge can also make the transition into musical theatre much easier and can help you to progress faster in your career.

All these years on, I have still not been able to find much of this information anywhere, in books or online. So I had the idea of compiling all the skills and knowledge that I had acquired over the last twenty-five years into a book in the hope that it could help other musicians who aspire to have a career in musical theatre, or at least have an interest in the subject. This book should give you some insight into the world of the show musician and guide you through the many skills needed to succeed in the industry. There is a lot you need to know to be a good show musician that goes way beyond just technical ability on your instrument; being a good player is only part of the job. This is not a book of technical exercises or technique — instead, it concentrates on the skills and knowledge needed to work in theatre that are rarely taught, even at music college or university, and that you could normally only learn on the job. You should have a better understanding of the many aspects of musical theatre, from how to get that first break to sustaining a long and successful career, as well as the environment, the equipment, and the personnel involved. More experienced musicians will inevitably have some knowledge of the subject matter, but my hope is that this book can benefit musicians of all levels of experience and musical ability. I also believe that much of the information can cross into other areas of work as a professional musician, regardless of whether they are in musical theatre or not.

Although my experience in musical theatre has been mainly based in the United Kingdom and on touring

Introduction

productions that originate in the UK, the information in this book is generally universal across all borders and productions. I do go into more detail on matters such as tax laws, which can be more specific to the UK, but the majority of the information will apply everywhere. When it comes to legal aspects of the profession such as contracts, tax regulation, and union agreements, make sure to check details in your locality to avoid any legal implications. I have done my best to include some of the more US-specific information and variants from the UK, i.e., different terms used on both sides of the Atlantic, but my advice is only a guideline, and I cannot take any responsibility for tax laws in each country or region.

If you aspire to or already work in musical theatre, I hope the information in this book will provide genuine value. Furthermore, I hope it will assist you in becoming a better musician and impart the knowledge and skills to help you to succeed in this very competitive industry. All information comes from my personal experiences of over twenty-five years as a freelance drummer and working in musical theatre. Additional information is provided by fellow musicians, as well as from research. If you have anything valuable to add or feel that a certain topic has not been covered, please go to www.showmusician.com or facebook.com/showmusician and leave a comment. By sharing our experiences and advice, we can hopefully build a community that can benefit all working musicians. Thank you.

1

The Skills Needed to Succeed

You need to have numerous skills if you want to succeed as a theatre musician. It's not enough to just be a great player. You also need to have excellent social skills and be very organised. You are self-employed and responsible for everything related to the life of a freelance musician, including timekeeping and finances. I have split these into two sections, personal and musical skills. Let's have a look at these in more detail.

PERSONAL SKILLS

Having certain personal skills and disciplines is crucial, not just when working as a musician but also in everyday life. As a professional in your craft, you need to maintain extremely high standards in all aspects of your professional life. Your conduct gives an important impression to the people around you, including your employer and potential future employers. Learn to keep the standards high and never let them slip. Many might think that this is obvious and take it for granted, but you'd be amazed how often this is overlooked, so read on and take on board what you need.

Punctuality

In musical theatre there are no excuses for being late — ever! Remember, there is normally no one to cover for you at short notice, and there may be two thousand people waiting in the audience to see a show. You don't want to be the one who holds up the performance or even gets it cancelled. Always leave plenty of time to get to the venue. Allow for traffic and public transport problems and have a back-up plan in case it all goes wrong. If you use public transport to get to work, ensure you have an alternative route planned using a different line or a bus route, or the option of getting in a car/taxi if necessary, and allowing enough time to make this happen. Does this sound overly careful? Believe me, the day will come when you will be glad that you planned ahead.

If touring, allow even more time, since the journeys are likely to be even longer. If you are flying to a venue, consider booking the flight prior to the one you need. This will ensure that you still have a following flight to get you there in time for the show should something happen.

On a rare occasion there may be an incident that is totally beyond your control, and you might not make the show. However, do everything in your power to make sure that doesn't happen. I have been performing for over twenty-five years and have never been late for a show or a gig, no matter what. Remember, no excuses! No one will care about the horrendous journey you may have had; they just care about the show starting on time. In most cases a lot of money is at stake, and one late arrival could have a negative impact on your reputation and even cost you your job.

The Show Musician

Attitude

Be a nice person. Smile and be positive. Get on with people and be social. Nobody likes someone who's constantly moaning and grumpy. It brings down the morale of the band and can also affect the musical chemistry of the players. Your reputation is everything in this industry, and you don't want to be known as someone who is a pain to be around. So act happy!

Appearance and Personal Hygiene

Your appearance is important and makes an impression. When at work, make sure that you are reasonably groomed and don't have any personal hygiene issues. The pit can be an intimate place, and no one wants it to be any less appealing than it already is. Take care of your personal appearance and make sure that your work clothes are clean and presentable.

Adaptability

Musical theatre draws on many musical styles and often jumps from one style to another within the course of a show. Musically, you must be comfortable dealing with that. You may also be asked to play something that is not written in the music. Often, last-minute changes are made and you need to be able to implement those quickly and confidently. Be ready for anything and try to be as accommodating as possible. Because of choreography, stage, and lighting cues, the music can at times appear to take a back seat, and what can seem like unmusical decisions can be made. You must try to see the bigger picture and realise that the music is just one part of a big and often complex production. Offer suggestions but

The Skills Needed to Succeed

remember that ultimately the conductor (also called a musical director or MD) and the musical supervisor (see Chapter 2) have the final word, and you will have to do the best you can to deliver on their vision, regardless of how you may feel about it.

Humility

Be humble. No one likes a big ego. You could be the most amazing player, but what everyone really cares about is that you play the show musically and consistently each and every time. No one cares about that lick or fill that you've spent ages practising. Everyone has worked hard to get to where they are, so give them their deserved respect and don't blow your own trumpet too much. Also, give compliments to other players where you feel they are deserved, but by the same token, be careful what you say to a band member if you feel they are not quite doing the music justice. Telling a musician that they are not up to the job can be counterproductive and can create a negative atmosphere in the band.

Organisation

You need to be extremely organised if you want to work as a freelance musician, whether it's in the world of theatre or elsewhere. You have to know where you need to be and when and be able to get there on time with all your necessary equipment. Nothing can be left to chance, because leaving behind just the smallest thing can be disastrous. So make sure that you get into the habit of being organised. I will go into this in more detail in the chapter 'Being Self-Employed.'

MUSICAL SKILLS

I believe you need to master a broad and varied set of musical skills to become a successful show musician. Being able to play your instrument to a high standard is only part of the story. Let's have a look at what I consider to be the most crucial elements.

Stylistic Knowledge

Because musical theatre touches on so many different styles of music, you need to have good knowledge of most genres of music — this is a point that gets reiterated throughout the book. Make sure that you study all major styles of music to a level where you can play and recognise them well. Listen to authentic music in every genre and if possible try to get experience playing the music in a live setting with a band. At the very least, practice playing along with the music until it feels comfortable. The more styles you can play, the more shows you can potentially do.

There is no substitute for playing with real musicians, so get out there and play every gig you possibly can — playing along with YouTube videos is not enough. Join that local rehearsal big band, do some hotel lobby jazz gigs, etc. These will all benefit you in building up your stylistic knowledge. Get some lessons from a teacher who is good in a particular style and soak up all the information they can give you. As a drummer I recommend learning at least one basic rhythm for each style well enough that you can play it from memory at any tempo. Whatever your instrument, make sure that you can play and that you familiarise yourself with the rhythms and harmony behind all major styles of music.

The Skills Needed to Succeed

Musical Styles You Need to Know

This list is by no means complete but more of a general list that you can expand upon.

- Rock & Pop
- Funk
- Disco
- Motown/Soul
- Modern Dance
- Reggae
- Country
- Blues
- Jazz Small Band (Bebop, Dixieland, etc.)
- Big Band Jazz
- Latin, including Brazilian, Cuban, and Caribbean styles

There are of course many more, so get exploring.

In the 'Other Useful Information' chapter you will find some more advice on essential listening you can use a starting point of your musical exploration.

Reading Skills

This is the subject many musicians worry about the most when they are looking at a career in musicals. Many think that they need to be able to faultlessly sight-read difficult pieces of music. With the exception of maybe an audition pianist, it is still possible to succeed in musical theatre even if you're not an amazing sight-reader. I am not undermining the importance of being a good reader; it's important, but you can still have a career in theatre even if your sight-reading isn't perfect.

You will in many cases get the music (which is sometimes referred to as the Pad or the Book) well in advance of playing the show, as well as a recording of the show, so you have plenty of time to work on any difficult parts you might have to play. It's more important that you are musical and can make a written piece of music sound good. Depending on the instrument you play, your part might be open to interpretation. Your musicality will come into play here, so make sure that you are familiar with the style of music that you are playing and of course make sure that you blend well with the other musicians in the band.

On the more traditional shows, the part might be intended to be played more literally. In this scenario you will need to make a judgement on how to approach your part. The musical director/conductor or musical supervisor may also insist on your part being played exactly like the written part. You will have to respect their decision and then try to make the most of the part, even if it's not particularly well arranged or inspiring.

That being said, I would highly recommend that you spend the time practising your reading, since it will help you immensely if you can make a part sound good quickly; often there are many other things to be thinking about as well as reading the music. Guitarists have to worry about programming sounds on pedals or digital racks and often changing instruments, like electric and acoustic guitars. Keyboard players have to worry about volume levels and patch changes, etc., and you will most likely be following a conductor as well.

How can you improve your reading skills? There is really only one way to improve your reading, and that is to do it. If you don't read music at all, get some lessons from a good teacher, buy some books, and get practising. There are many great books out there now for all instruments, which include recordings of music, accompanied by charts that mimic professional written music. This is a great way to practise what you might encounter in the real world. There are also many useful online tutorials, and you can do grades in music theory. Whichever path you decide to take, don't forget that there is no substitute for real-world experience. Get out there and find bands that require you to read music. Things like your local rehearsal big band, local brass band, etc. See what's out there. Just remember that reading music alone is not enough; you also need to be a good listener and be familiar with the style of music that you are playing. This will help to bring musicality and authenticity to the music and ultimately make you sound better. The key is to start slowly and make sure that you understand everything in the part, then build up speed. Don't let your reading skills stop you — get out there, and your reading will improve the more you do it.

Tip

- Practise with a backing track
- Practice with a click/metronome
- Transcribe music yourself from recordings
- Listen to music that comes with charts and follow the music carefully. This will help to develop your reading speed.

The way music is written for each instrument can be very different. Rhythmic phrases can also be written in different ways, so try to expose yourself to as many different charts as possible. This will help you prepare for any eventuality. Also, make sure that you read consistently, since it's easy to get out of practice. Try to read something every day to keep your chops up to scratch.

Reading music is about much more than just reading the notes. The real skill in reading music well is to be able to turn notes on a page into a piece of music that both sounds good and works in the context of what the other musicians around you are playing. Interpretation of your part is crucial on any instrument, but probably more so for rhythm section instruments, where the parts can often be more of a guide than a literal part. Even though dynamics and articulation are often written in to help the musician make the part more musical, you still need to be able to react and blend with the other instruments, adding to the musical unity that the composer can't express on paper. You don't just play the notes; you make them musical by using your judgement and musicality to add inflections and phrasing. This is what makes it a piece of music and not just notes on a page. Don't get too engrossed in reading the notes; try to envisage the end product. The written music is a tool — good music is the end goal.

Musicality

I talk about musicality a lot in this book. There is a good reason for this. I think musicality is the most important thing when it comes to playing your instrument. It's what turns black dots on a page into music as well as the collective collaboration of musicians (a band) that can move the audience on an emotional level. Musicality is what separates a good musician from a great one. Two players might have equal technical ability on their instrument, but it's how you apply that to the music that matters. This is what I think gives the player their edge or that X-factor.

I look at musicality as the little nuances and musical knowledge a player brings to a piece. There is a big difference between just playing a piece of music and playing with feeling and a true knowledge of what makes that style of music feel good, often referred to as groove, swing, or the pocket, depending on the style. These terms all mean the same thing in essence; it means that the music feels good, which in turn brings an emotional and physical experience. It is what makes the listener want to move their body, tap their feet, laugh, or cry. Music is a very powerful medium, but the player has to have the skill and musical understanding to portray that to the listener. This goes for individuals as well as whole bands. For the music to feel good, everyone in the band needs to be on the same page and approach the music the same way, and of course listen to each other. It only takes one member of a band to be out of sync to kill the groove.

So how do you develop this skill? In this there are no shortcuts. The key is to listen to music, every style, every genre, whether you like the music or not. Only when you are familiar with the style and are able to play it well can you bring that authenticity, and, more importantly, feel and groove to the music. So listen and play along to different styles of music and try to understand the feel and the essence of each style. Check out the most influential players in each style on your instrument, analyse their playing, and try to copy what they are doing. What makes their playing unique, and how do they approach their instrument for that style? Looking into the history and back catalogue of certain styles can also often help in better understanding the music. How did this style originate, and how did it develop? What was the music for? Is it for telling stories, for dancing, is it laid-back or driving, etc.?

Working With a Band

Being able to work well with a group of musicians is a necessary skill when working in musical theatre. You need to be able to get on both musically and personally. The situation in a pit environment can often be very unsocial and unmusical. You often can't see the other band members because of the space limitations and screening used, and with

The Skills Needed to Succeed

the use of personal monitoring it is often difficult to hear and judge things like band dynamics. Your best friend is without a doubt your ears in this situation.

Your monitoring mix is crucial, so spend time getting it right so that you can hear everyone in the band. Be sensitive to other instruments and try to blend musically and not to overplay. In an ideal situation, every member of the band understands the music well and fits well together as a unit, in which case things should happen pretty easily and the music should settle quickly, with everyone in the band playing their parts well and the music grooving away. Unfortunately, this is not always the case, and I will discuss how to deal with this in more detail later on.

The key things to consider when playing in a band are:

- Listening: Listen carefully to every instrument and the vocals.

- Phrasing: Try to phrase your part in line with the rest of the band.

- Dynamics: Adjust your dynamics with the band. (This can be difficult in a pit situation. I will go into that later in the 'Working in a Pit Environment' chapter.)

- Musicality: Don't overplay, and be as stylistically accurate as possible.

- Timekeeping: You need to sit with the band and have consistent time, otherwise the music will not groove.

Note

Recording your performance is a great way to check how you sit with the other musicians and the overall sound of the show. Hearing your performance in context while not immersed in playing can also give you some ideas on how you could potentially improve your part. Try to get a balanced mix as close as you think it should sound if heard from the audience's perspective. Do a test recording and then listen and adjust until a decent balance is achieved using a second pit-monitoring mixer. (See 'Working in a Pit Environment' chapter)

Consistency

In musical theatre, consistency is crucial, both mentally and musically. No one cares if you're having a bad day. Make sure to leave all your personal issues at the door and perform a good show, every show. Also, as mentioned earlier, try to be consistently positive and happy. We all have good days and bad days, but learn to put on a happy face and get on with the job. With experience you can make even your worst performance sound like a good one. Remember, you are there

The Skills Needed to Succeed

to do a job, which is to make the show sound good and the same every time.

Consistency in your playing is important for many reasons. You need to remember that there are more than just the musicians around you listening to your playing. There are numerous cast members who might be taking cues from your playing, unbeknownst to you, as well as lighting cues and stage cues, so you need play the show pretty much identical every time. If you start adding drastically different fills or straying away from your normal part, you might be throwing someone off, onstage or off, which could seriously impact the show. There are many people who work on a musical production: cast, stage crew, and technical teams, and we all need to work as a team. Stay musical, stay consistent, and try to envisage the show as a whole.

Working With a Click

The majority of shows will have some use of a click (i.e., a metronome), and many are entirely clicked. You have to be extremely comfortable playing with a click, since you will most definitely be hearing it in your ear throughout your career as a show musician. The only way to get comfortable with a click is to practise with one and make it your friend. Learn to sit with the click, but at the same time don't become a slave to it; we still want to sound like human beings.

Note

For those of you who may not know what a click is, it is essentially a digital metronome that you will hear in your monitor mix, and you have to play in time with it. This metronome can be linked to pre-recorded music, such as additional instrumental parts, extra vocals, and sound effects, etc., in the show. This is often referred to as a 'Backing Track,' 'Click Track,' or just 'The Track.'

So why is click used so much on shows? Do they not trust us musicians to keep time? Well, yes and no. There are numerous reasons why there is so much click being used these days.

1. There are other instruments on track, and backing vocals, etc., so it needs to be clicked so that the band can lock in with that.

2. The creative team, choreographer, director, etc., want the tempos to be exactly the same every night so that the show looks and feels the same every time.

3. There could be some automation on stage that has to be synced to the music, so a click is used to keep it in sync.

4. All of the above.

Points 1 and 2 are the most common, and what gets put on the track varies depending on the show and instrumentation. Instruments like percussion and strings are commonly put on track, and also extra vocals to fill out the sound coming from the stage. There are also instances where a show is very dance-led, and the singers just can't physically sing at their best while doing intense dance moves onstage, so their vocal gets doubled on the track. On some shows the click is there purely as a timekeeper and to keep the tempos exactly the same every show. Many shows have the main songs clicked, and some of the underscore (where you play under dialog) is not clicked so that the conductor/musical director can pull the tempo around a little to fit with the action on stage. In some instances using instruments on track has also become a way for the producers to reduce costs by reducing the number of musicians in the band, which is something that unions continually campaign against. Hopefully this will not get worse, and the number of band members in the pit will start to increase again.

It can be frustrating always to have a click in your ear, and the feel and groove of a song can suffer because of it, especially if the tempo has been set where it feels either too slow or too fast for the particular song. With a click, the musicians can't do anything to alter the tempo, even if it would work much better musically. However, as long as the band works as a unit, working with a click is usually pretty painless, and you get used to it quickly.

Tip

If the show has a rhythm section, you can try to turn the click down in your monitor mix so that it blends in with the music more. Use the drummer and rhythm section as your timekeeper and don't worry too much about the click. It will make the music more enjoyable to play and feel more natural. However, if you're the drummer, you'll need that click in your monitor, loud and clear!

Having a click can also be a blessing, especially if you're the drummer or the conductor. You don't have to worry about whether you have the tempo right, since it's always dictated, and it stops any arguments from dancers and choreographers when they start complaining that a particular song was too slow this evening. This is normally due to them having a bit more energy that evening or a few too many coffees before the show.

Working Without a Click and Timekeeping

Then there are, of course, the shows that don't have any click, or very little. One of the possible downsides of playing frequently with a click is that when you have to play without one, it can make you a little unsure of your own timekeeping abilities. Therefore, you also have to work on your own timekeeping skills, since you can't always rely on a click, the drummer, or the conductor to keep you in time. The way to do that is to practise both with and without a click. A good way to test yourself is to program a click into a computer and then add in silenced bars where the click drops out. Start with one bar, then increase it to two and four, and so on, and see if you can keep time and come in again with the click. You can do this using programs like GarageBand or Logic on a Mac or Cubase or equivalent on a PC. There are also apps available for iPhones and Android devices. If you are unfamiliar with this software, you can check out YouTube for instructional tutorials to get you started.

If you are used to playing more song-based music, you will be accustomed to tempos staying consistent throughout the song. In musical theatre, you will often find that tempo will change and fluctuate throughout a piece. These can sometimes be very sudden changes between sections or more of a gradual change. It is common for songs to gradually speed up throughout. This is usually done to build a sense of energy through the song, but it can feel unnatural to play, especially when playing music that is more rock-oriented. It can be useful to try to practise dealing with sudden tempo changes and to be more aware of tempos in general, especially as a rhythm player.

If you are setting the tempo for a show that does not use a click, it's a good rule to check yourself before the show against a metronome; this goes for conductors and drummers alike. Tempo is a very organic thing, and you can feel the same tempo differently from one day to the next, depending on your state of mind, if you're tired, or had a lot of caffeine. So check if you're having a slow or a fast day, and then you will at least be aware of it and can adjust accordingly. I often warm up before the show using a metronome with the tempo of the first song of the show to give me a reference. I can then judge if I am feeling the tempo correctly that day. Find what works for you. It's important to be consistent in your playing, including your timekeeping.

The Backing Track

It's becoming more and more popular to use backing tracks on shows. As mentioned earlier, this is done for numerous reasons but is most commonly used to fill out the arrangement by adding extra instruments and vocals. When backing tracks are used, you have to be sensitive to this, and you may need to adapt your playing to be in sync with what's on the track. When there are other instruments on the track that are in a similar tonal register to your own instrument, you need to make sure that you are not clashing. Sometimes instruments even get doubled on tracks. When this happens, make sure that you are in tune with the track, since this can vary ever so slightly, depending on how the track was created, and most often the track can't be changed that easily. Also, be aware of any rhythmic clashes that could happen and adapt your playing accordingly.

As a rule, just make sure that you can hear the track clearly and don't just ignore it, since this can potentially sound horrendous out front if the track is mixed high in the overall mix. You need be aware of what is happening on the track and try and make it as musical as possible. This can be frustrating when what's on the track is not all that inspiring, but if you make the necessary musical adjustments, you can potentially make it sound better. Have a discussion with your MD early on if you notice any clashes with the track, and try to fix the issue. As soon as a show is up and running, it can be much more difficult to address.

Dynamics

The use of dynamics is extremely important in musicals, and they are used extensively. Most musicals have much more light and shade dynamically than, for instance, pop or rock songs. Make sure that you can play your instrument well at all dynamic levels and be aware of how it affects the feel or sound of your instrument so you have the necessary control and skill when called upon.

The problem you may encounter in a pit situation when dealing with dynamics and volume is the monitoring. With musicians often being split up and screened off, it can be difficult to judge the overall dynamics of the band as you would in a standard onstage band setup using acoustic monitoring. With in-ear monitors thrown into the mix, it becomes a virtually impossible task. If you play an acoustic instrument, you will have to rely on your own relative volume to try to blend with the rest of the band, while electronic instruments like keyboards will usually have volume meters to gauge their volume. The overall mix, as heard by the audience, is adjusted by the sound operator.

The use of in-ear monitoring has now become common practise in most musical situations, from studio work to party bands, so you are likely to get some experience of this before doing your first musical theatre gig. The truth of it is that most musicians in musical theatre, and in fact any musicians who use in-ear monitoring, never really know what they or the band as a whole truly sound like to the audience. The only exception is the MD, who will have the chance to listen to the show from out front. We have to live with what we hear in our monitoring, since it is the only reference we have, and accept that we are very much at the mercy of the sound operators when it comes to the dynamics and the overall balance of the band or orchestra, as heard from the audience's perspective. This also means that every member of the band will have a slightly different impression of the band's sound, depending on his or her mix in their monitoring. You just have to imagine and hope that it sounds great out front and play the best show you can every time.

Confidence

Always act confident and give the impression that you are well prepared and capable of doing the job, no matter what the situation. When you do a show for the first time, you will undoubtedly be nervous, which is only natural and expected. However, you still need to portray confidence in what you are doing. If you have done your preparations for the show, you should feel confident in your ability to play, even if you are extremely nervous. Don't give your fellow musicians any reasons to question your ability to play the show, especially the MD. The MD needs to feel assured that you are going to play confidently. It doesn't matter if it's your first or your hundredth performance of a show, if you've had a bad day or have the flu — you need to go in there and play with the same quality as your best performance. So when you arrive for your show, and in fact any performance, make sure that you hide your nervousness and act in a humble but professional and confident way.

Truly believing in your own ability is important, but no matter how good you are at your instrument, nothing can

The Skills Needed to Succeed

substitute for good preparation. I go into this in more detail in Chapter 3, but make sure that you are always as prepared as you possibly can be and that you know that show inside out. Then you can be truly confident in your playing and give a great performance every time.

2

How to Get Work in Musical Theatre

This is of course the question to which everyone wants a response, but unfortunately I don't think there's a definitive answer. Everyone's story is slightly different in how they started out in musical theatre and show work. However, everyone that has made a career out of it has one thing in common: when the first opportunity came along to play a show, they were prepared and had honed their skills to a high enough standard to do a good job.

I suppose my story is like that of many musicians I know who now work in theatre. I ironically had no ambition to work in theatre to begin with. I was a freelance player and was doing the rounds with different bands, doing functions and studio work. I was doing a gig with a party band, and a keyboard player, a friend of one of the band members, saw me play and got my number. Six months later I get a call from him; he had recommended me to the drummer on the show that he was working on at the time, and from that I got my first dep in theatre. (A 'dep' is short for deputy and is when you cover for the regular player on a show. In the US it is called 'a sub,' which is short for substitute — this is covered in more detail later on in this chapter). I must have done an okay job, because what followed was show after show, and I was working full-time in musical theatre. The way you get your first break can come in many different ways, but what is important is that you do the groundwork and are ready for it when it happens. We talked about the many skills you need to master in the previous chapter. Now let's have a look at what you can do to get your name out there and what else you can do to get yourself prepared for that first break.

GET OUT THERE!

You first and foremost need to get out there and play. Get as much experience as you can in as many musical situations as possible and hone your skills as a player until you are confident playing in most situations. Working with numerous musicians in different environments will give you the experience you need for working on shows, and the more people you meet and hear you play, the more likely it is that someone will recommend you down the line. Make sure you are always super prepared for any gig you do, no matter how insignificant you think it is, because you never know who you might meet at a function gig or a pub gig, or who might be watching. In this business your reputation is everything!!! So get out there!

NETWORKING

Networking is crucial to get work in theatre or indeed any profession. It doesn't matter how great a player you may be if no one knows about you! There are many ways to network these days. Social media is booming, and new services are coming along all the time. However, I find that meeting people face-to-face and letting your personality, and most importantly, your playing do the talking is by far the best way to get your name out in the music community. Another way to meet fellow musicians, especially in theatre, is to sit in. This gets covered in more detail later on in this chapter, but basically you contact a player on a show, and you go and sit next to them while they play the show. This is a great way to see how it all works and of course to meet fellow players. However, this is not a ticket to a job or a dep.

Tip

Some people take networking to a level where it starts to become a nuisance and in turn gives them a reputation of being 'a networker' or being pushy, which is something you don't want. Be respectful and tactful; there can be a fine line between getting to know people using social media and social stalking.

SELF-PROMOTION

Social Media

There are many tools available these days to get your name out. Social media is without a doubt the most popular medium to do this with services such as Facebook, Twitter, LinkedIn, and others. These are sites where you can follow what other musicians are up to and can be a good way to find out about gigs and jam nights in your area. You can also get involved in discussions online, but just make sure that you do it in a sensible way to avoid crossing that line of social media stalking. Start by signing up with the most popular social media services and then try to be active by updating often with relevant posts.

A Personal Website

Having your own website can be beneficial and a great place to direct people to see what you are up to and your experience. It's relatively easy to set up a professional-looking website. Depending on your computer skills, you can use free services like WordPress to create a good-looking website; however, you will need hosting to get it online, and you will need to purchase a domain name for your site. Domain names like www.yourname.com, www.yourname.co.uk, or similar work well if you are promoting yourself, and you can check what's available and purchase a domain with numerous services online. Just Google 'domain name' and choose one that works for you. You can in most cases also purchase hosting through the same provider with which you have your domain name. Some of the popular ones are GoDaddy, 1and1, and NameCheap, but there are many more.

> **Note**
>
> Hosting is the space you need to keep your website online so that people can access it. Your site will be stored on the web servers of the provider you choose, which basically puts it in the cloud. It can then be found with search

engines like Google, and of course by typing in your domain name.

You can also create a website using a piece of software on your computer instead of using WordPress, but I do find that cost of the software and the learning curve to learn to use the software is not worth it, unless you are planning on creating numerous websites.

An even easier way is to use a service like Squarespace or Weebly to create your website. They offer a one-stop solution. You can buy your domain name through them, which is included in the price, and they handle all the hosting for you. You just sign up, choose a template you like, and then drag and drop your content into it. It will most likely work out a little more expensive than using WordPress and separate hosting, but it can be worth it for convenience, and you are guaranteed to get a great-looking website that works on both desktop and mobile devices. You can of course also hire a web designer who can do all this for you, but the cost of that will be much higher.

Your website is a reflection of you, so try to create something that suits your image. Make sure that it is simple and easy to navigate. Having good graphics is crucial, so see if you can get a friend who is good with a camera to take some photos of you with your instrument, or you can find great stock images online, if you prefer not to use your own photos. Just make sure that you don't use any photos that are copyrighted. You can pay for high-quality photos with online services like Getty Images and Shutterstock, among others.

Have some information about yourself on there and possibly your CV with your experience. Having your schedule on there is a good idea, especially if you are on a show or have a busy schedule. If your diary is reasonably empty at this stage, maybe don't advertise that fact too much. If you offer teaching, you can promote that on your website, and also any other services you might offer. You can even put up audio and video of your performances for people to see. Just make sure that they are of a high standard; a poor-quality recording or video can be counterproductive. Photos and links to other relevant websites, and even a blog, is something you can also consider. Check out other websites for inspiration.

Instead of a personal webpage, or in addition to one, you can also create a Facebook business page. This can act as website for your professional life, and you can post your schedule and other information there. It will never look quite as nice as a personal website, but it can be a good place to start. You can create a page directly from your personal account on Facebook or just search for Facebook Business for more information online.

Your CV/Resume

Your CV (Curriculum Vitae) or Resume is something that you need to get sorted early on. Musicians rarely ask for another musician's CV when booking for a gig, since most things are done via word of mouth recommendations. However, the fixers and musical contractors will on most occasions ask for one. Even if you haven't got much to put on your CV early on, you can keep adding to it as you acquire more gigs and experience in your career.

Your CV/Resume needs to have the following information:

- Your name
- Contact details, including your email and website, if you have one
- Your music-related experience in chronological order, with the most recent first
- Your music-related education, including music grades and qualifications
- Any other information like driving license and languages you can include if you wish
- A couple of references are good to have. This is the name and contact details of someone who knows you personally and has preferably worked with you in a musical setting. If you put someone down as a reference, make sure that you contact them first and ask if it's okay to do that, since they may be contacted directly about your CV. If they have no idea that they are references, it may reflect badly on you.

Keep the CV clear, with just your name and contact details at the top. Don't put a photograph of yourself or try to do anything adventurous with the formatting; plain and simple is fine. Follow your contact details with your work experience, then list the gigs you have done, including any relevant information, but keep it short. Your CV should never be more than two pages of A4 or letter size. One page is ideal, since many people will only ever read the first page.

At the very least keep the most relevant information on the first page.

Cover Letter

Every time you send out a CV, you also need to accompany that with a cover letter. Your CV will usually stay consistent, although you can do minor adjustments to make it more suited to certain jobs, but the cover letter is unique to the person you are sending it to. The cover letter would be written in the main body of an email, and the CV should then be attached as a PDF or Word document. In your cover letter you address the person you are sending it to personally, and you include information about yourself that is relevant to the work you are after. Don't make it longer than a couple of paragraphs and try and sell yourself as being suitable for the position and show real enthusiasm and excitement, without being over the top. Remember to attach that CV, to check for spelling mistakes, and to include your contact details on the email. If you get a reply, respond quickly and always be polite. If you don't get a reply within a week or two, send a friendly follow-up email to double-check that they received your previous email.

LONDON - NEW YORK

Many musicians I meet think that the only way to get work is to move to the big city. This is not necessarily the case, although you might need to move within a commutable distance of the city at some point if your career takes off. The mistake many musicians make is to pick up sticks and move to the centre of London or New York without having any work lined up or even any contacts. This is not advisable

The Show Musician

unless you already have another income stream, since renting and living in these cities is astronomically expensive. What often happens is that people run out of money very quickly without having had the necessary time to build up any work or reputation and are forced to move back home, broke, to their parents. What you need to do is plan well and budget for at least six months to a year, if you want to do this.

There are many ways to build up your reputation without moving into the centre of the theatre hub. While living at home, start building your presence on social media by posting about local gigs you are doing. Contact touring musicians who are in your city and see if you can sit in with them. Get experience with local theatre companies and get some shows under your belt, and do as many gigs as you can and meet other musicians. Use any contacts you have to try and get a dep on a touring show. This will help to give you a profile with the big fixers/musical contractors who also hire musicians for shows in the West End or on Broadway (depending on which side of the Atlantic you live), or wherever in the world you are located.

Tip

It can be easy to get labelled either as a 'touring player' or a 'town player' by the fixers and musical contractors. If you are serious about working in the West End or on Broadway, you need to be on the scene for that to happen. Think carefully about taking on long tours or disappearing off the scene for any length of time. Although some musicians do both touring and town work, you can easily be forgotten.

Make trips to the city to check out some shows and try to get a sit-in with some of the players there. This will help to get your name out a little more. Try to get in touch with players through a contact if you can; for instance, someone you may know on the show. If you contact the player cold, just remember to be courteous and explain that you are interested in getting into musical theatre, and if it would be possible to come and check out the show for some experience. Never ask if you can come and dep for them. Make contact first and build some sort of relationship. The chance is that they will only offer you a dep/sub if you have been recommended to them by another musician that they trust. There are also other factors, which I will go into later. If you feel ready to take on the big city, budget very carefully and try to share accommodation with other musicians if possible. This will lower your costs, and you will have some support and company, which can be invaluable. Another way is to go as a student and use the time while doing your studies to get your name about the town, but this has other issues like funding your studies and being accepted into a college or university in the city (see below).

Try to find popular jam nights where you can showcase your playing. Find out where musicians hang out after the shows, and come down and be social. Try to join some local function bands, rehearsal big bands, or whatever you can find. Many of the show musicians will also do function bands and other work to break up the monotony of the show, so you can make some important connections on that random wedding gig.

You could also consider moving to a smaller town just outside the city, where you can either drive in or use public transport to get into the city centre. Outside the city, accommodation will be considerably cheaper and the pace of life slightly less manic, which might suit you better. Just check that you can always get back home late at night on public transport and that the cost of travel isn't more than you can afford.

If it is your ambition to work as a musician in the theatre hubs of London or New York, the chance is that you will have to move closer to the city when you start working regularly and your reputation builds. Also, remember that many musicians make a decent living outside of the big cities, either on touring shows or doing other freelance work. You just have to decide what you want to do and where you want to take your career.

EDUCATION

Do you need a degree in music to work in musical theatre? The simple answer is no, you don't, but it can be beneficial in many regards to do some sort of further education in music, and it can help push your playing to a higher level. One of the biggest benefits you may get from a music course is the contacts you will make. From my personal experience, this was the most valuable benefit I got from doing a degree in music. Many of the gigs I have done as a professional came from a connection I made at university. I believe it is possible to learn all the necessary skills we have talked about without doing a music degree, but it can potentially accelerate your learning curve. You will have to weigh the benefits and cost to decide if this is a path you would like to take.

If you decide you want to do a music degree, or further education of some sort, do your research well on courses available and how you could possibly fund your studies. Student loans are often available, but make sure you take living expenses into consideration as well. Go to open days at the institutions you are interested in and check out the facilities. Try to speak with current students about their experience and also check out who will be teaching you on your instrument. I would always recommend studying with a teacher who is an active player as well as a teacher. They can give you up-to-date real-world advice and even recommend you for some gigs down the line.

Fixers (UK)/
Musical Contractors (US)

What are fixers or musical contractors? This is something pretty unique to theatre, and when I started out I didn't have a clue what a fixer was. Basically a fixer 'fixes the band,' which means they are in charge of booking the musicians for a specific musical theatre production. A 'musical contractor,' or sometimes musical coordinator, is the title used in the States, but it is essentially the same as a fixer; they contract the band.

Note

In the US you will most likely be dealing with the house contractor. This is a salaried position and is usually a member of the orchestra or band. Their job is to do the weekly payroll, hand out paycheques, and keep track of any substitutes being used. They are also the port-of-call for any information on contractual matters. In the UK a deputy supervisor is sometimes appointed who will coordinate the use of deputies but will not usually handle things like payroll.

The producers will have a budget for the music and an idea of how many musicians are needed and what instruments need to be used for a particular show. They contact the fixer/contractor with whom they normally work, and they then book the musicians they think are the most suitable for the job. However, a musical supervisor normally gets booked first, and they will have a say in who they want on the gig, and then a musical director/conductor is booked, who will also have a say in who they want booked. So, often, the fixer does not have that much of a say, depending on how demanding the musical supervisor and the MD are on getting 'their guys.' The fixers will have many musicians on their books and always try to use players they trust and have used before, and they have the power to say to an MD or supervisor, 'I will not use this player,' because of whatever reason. The message here is don't piss off a fixer!

How to Get Work in Musical Theatre

As you can see, there are a lot of people involved in choosing players for a show, so it can be very hard for a newcomer to get in. This is especially true for rhythm section players, since MDs often want players they know. The fixer is also your point of call on a show you're working on if you have any issues. I would, however, always go to the MD first with any problems, unless they *are* the problem. The fixer in most cases handles the payroll for the musicians and needs to approve any time off and sometimes sit-ins. See the 'Taking Time Off a Show' section for more details on how that works and the protocols that are often used.

Note

Although the majority of commercial shows use a fixer, there are some exceptions to this. Some shows will choose to book musicians directly, which is often referred to as 'in-house.' All the payroll and organising of musicians will then be handled by the producer and their team, and no middleman is used. This system is also common on the slightly lower-budget shows that tour the country, as well as in independent and smaller theatres in London. Countries like Germany also do not traditionally use a fixer; the band will in most cases be booked by the musical director.

All that being said, it can be worth contacting fixers/musical contractors directly. They are often looking for players for many different shows and can take a chance on a player that they haven't used before, providing you have some relevant experience. On occasion there might even be auditions for musicians on certain shows, although this is rare. Find out who the fixers are in your area and send them your details with your CV, as we talked about earlier. You never know what might come of it, and it could raise your profile a little with the fixers. Just be careful not to be too persistent with emails and phone calls.

MUSICAL SUPERVISOR

Musical supervisors should not be confused with the previously discussed musical contractor (although on some occasions the same person could cover both roles). They are normally in charge of anything music-related on a production. They will often choose the MD and even many of the musicians for the band, although normally the MD's opinion will be asked. So, knowing the musical supervisor of a show can be good way to get your name in the running for the band. A musical supervisor has on some occasions worked on a previous version of the show before so is therefore classed as an expert on how the show should sound. Some are more involved than others, and you may only ever see them in the odd rehearsal and possibly the band calls at the early stages of a show. Sometimes the musical supervisor is also the MD of the show and will therefore stay with the show throughout the run. I will go into more details in the 'Who's Who in Theatre' chapter about each person's role in the musical theatre machine.

Musical Director (MD)/Conductor

The MD or conductor is another person who can be extremely influential in which musician gets chosen for a show. MDs are most commonly keyboard players, so it can be useful to get friendly with any keyboard player you might work with, since they may eventually became theatre MDs. I don't, however, recommend trying to create superficial friendships with the single-minded goal of getting work. This will undoubtedly backfire in the long run, but it's worth it to at least stay in touch through social media or other means. I will go into more detail about the MD's role later in the book.

Your Reputation

In this industry your reputation is hugely important. When you are offered a show, as a dep or as the regular player, do some background work on the show before committing to make sure that you are capable of playing it well. Don't take on shows, or in fact any work, unless you are confident you will do a good job. Reputation spreads quickly and is difficult to restore. If you do take on a job that's outside your comfort zone, make sure you do your homework.

Things to remember

- Do your homework. Know that show inside out.
- Know your tempos and tempo changes well (drummers especially).
- Video the MD if possible when learning the show (make sure you ask permission before doing this).
- Know your weaknesses.

Amateur Theatre

There are amateur theatre companies and smaller non-commercial theatres in most major cities. These will put on productions throughout the year and will often need musicians. Do some research about theatre companies in your area and send them your CV/resume. You can gain some valuable experience doing small productions like these and also make some good contacts for future work. However, the budgets can often be small, and the pay for musicians reflects that, with only money for expenses being offered at times. If you are starting out, this can be an option to gain experience, but just make sure you are not being exploited.

Cruise Ships

Working on cruise ships can be a great experience in so many ways. Many musicians who work in musical theatre started their careers working on a cruise ship or have worked on ships at some time. You can get some show experience playing the numerous productions on the ships, which are now often truncated versions of West End and Broadway shows. You also have much variety, since you will often be backing the many different cabaret acts that tour the cruise ships, plus you might be doing many of the party nights that the cruise staff put on. This amount of musical variety is also great for your reading skills. Although the money paid on ships is often rather poor, you still get to travel the world while being paid for it, and it's in most cases tax-free income. So if you get the opportunity to work on a cruise ship, go for it.

Check the Internet for cruise work. Some cruise liners use agencies to book their musicians, while others do it in-house. Some of the major cruise companies are:

- The Carnival Corporation, which owns Carnival Cruises, Cunard, Costa, Holland America, Seabourn, Aida Cruises, P&O Cruises, and Princess Cruises
- Royal Caribbean Cruises
- Celebrity Cruises
- Fred Olsen Cruise Lines
- Disney Cruises
- Norwegian Cruise Line

and many more.

PANTOMIMES

Pantomimes are a bit of a UK-based phenomenon and don't, as far as I'm aware, exist anywhere else in the world, at least in the format done in the UK. If you've never seen a pantomime, you are in for a treat, because it's probably not like anything you'll have seen before. Pantomimes are put on over the Christmas period in the UK in all major towns around the country. Some of the bigger towns will even have numerous pantos running in the city at the same time. They are essentially shows for children but with some subtle (or even not so subtle) adult humour thrown in. A panto will usually run from late November or start of December to January, or even into February.

The Show Musician

Some pantomimes are put on by big production companies and can be high-budget spectacles starring international stars. Lower-budget versions are also popular, and they tend to follow a more traditional style format. In the UK there are a few big production companies that specialise in pantomimes. The most notable are Qdos, First Family Entertainment, and UK Productions, and they put on pantos in some of the biggest theatres in the UK, often with big international stars as well as top UK celebrities.

The format of a pantomime is a fairytale story done in a more lighthearted and humorous way, with big musical numbers of recent popular songs and well-known songs from Disney movies, etc. The most common of the fairytales used are *Aladdin, Jack and the Beanstalk, Cinderella, Peter Pan, Snow White, Dick Whittington,* and *Sleeping Beauty*. What makes the pantomimes slightly unusual is the fact that there is usually a gender swap in the roles, with men playing some of the leading female characters, like the ugly sisters in *Cinderella*, for instance, and sometimes the lead male is played by a girl, like in *Peter Pan*. This is an old tradition of pantomimes, which is thought to have originated from old Italian comedy plays. If you grew up living in the UK, there is every chance you will have seen a pantomime or two.

As a musician in the UK, doing a pantomime can be a great way to break into the theatre scene and get some experience. Many professional show musicians will do pantos at Christmas and often try to secure their most local panto to home, and then do it year after year for guaranteed work over the Christmas period. Pantomimes don't usually use independent fixers like the normal theatre shows but are usually fixed in-house. The bigger production houses, as mentioned earlier, will have a musical supervisor who will also deal with fixing the band. On the smaller pantos it will most likely be the MD that will fix the band, although they may inherit a number of players that do that particular pantomime year after year.

To get a job on a pantomime, it can be a good idea to send your CV and cover letter to the musical supervisors of the bigger production companies, since they will often struggle finding people to cover all of the shows they need to fix, so you might get lucky. However, as with most shows, they will usually use recommendations from other musicians that they know and trust to find new musicians for their shows. So, as mentioned before, you need get out there and get your name out. As well as contacting the big production companies, also find out where your local pantos are and contact them directly. Get the contact details for the musical supervisor or MD and send them your info. You should be able to find most information online, or you can call the theatres directly.

Pantomimes can pay decent money, but the schedule is hectic. There are usually a few days of technical rehearsals, just as with most other shows, and there will also be a rehearsal period prior to that, which the MD will be a part of. There is usually not an assistant MD involved on a panto, so the MD's job can be a busy one. On the bigger pantos the rehearsals will often take place in London and then move to the performing theatre, while the smaller productions will most likely rehearse local to the venue. When the show is up and running, you can expect to be doing at least ten to twelve shows a week, so basically two shows a day, six days a week. Some pantos have morning shows, while others have more usual times of an afternoon matinee and an evening show. Some pantos may even do three shows in a day, morning, afternoon, and evening. Whatever it is, you can expect a very busy schedule for the duration of the panto season.

You may find that there are strict rules when it comes to taking time off a pantomime. This is particularly the case with rhythm section players and especially drummers. In fact, drummers are often totally forbidden from taking any time off a panto. This is because their role is often very integral to the action on the stage, since they are expected to play sound effects in time with what is happening onstage. They will usually take their cues directly from the performers as well as the MD, so their part can be difficult to learn quickly, if a dep needs to come in to cover. Just make sure you ask about time-off rules before taking on the contract so that it's clear and doesn't cause you issues down the line.

It's common to offer musicians a buyout on pantos rather than to pay on a show-to-show basis. This is often a set weekly fee or even an all-in fee for the entire run. This will include any band calls, rehearsals, sound checks, and shows. This will in most cases also include any subsistence and accommodation if you are working away from home, and possibly even travel. Remember, on a buyout there will be no extras for extra calls or overtime. If you get a buyout offer, just double-check the amount against the schedule and the hours that you are expected to work. Also, make sure you ask what is included so it is clear. If you are away from home, remember to ask about travel and subsistence, since this can sometimes be negotiated. Just make sure that by the time you've accounted for accommodation and travel costs, you are not working for a pittance in relation to the hours worked. You can always go the union for advice if need be.

Contact details:

Qdos Pantomimes: www.qdosentertainment.co.uk

First Family Entertainment: www.ffe-uk.com

UK Productions: www.ukproductions.co.uk

THE DEP/THE SUB

The word 'dep' is short for deputy, used in the UK, and 'sub' is short for substitute, which is the term commonly used in the US, and is referred to as depping or subbing.

This is one of the most important ways to build your reputation in theatre. This is where you get a chance to cover for another player on a show, and you get to prove yourself in a show environment. This can, however, often be a baptism of fire, as I'll explain further in the next chapter. Even if you haven't been offered a dep, it's a good idea to contact players on shows and go and sit in with them just to see how it's done and to get used to the environment in the pit. This is where you sit behind the regular player and watch them play the show. Just never assume that by sitting in you will be offered a dep. Unless the player knows you or you have been recommended to them by someone they trust, you will not be offered a dep. And remember that you will have to be approved by the MD and often the fixer, so don't assume there is a quick and easy way to get in. You could be the best player in town, but unless you have been recommended, you will most likely not be asked. Whatever you do, don't pester a musician about sitting in. It's very easy to get a reputation for being a 'networker' or being 'pushy,' so make sure you go in with the right attitude and respect. Remember that most musicians in theatre have gigged for years, done numerous deps, and have a built a reputation, so don't insult them by expecting just to be handed a job as a deputy or a substitute.

The way most musicians, including myself, got into theatre was by gigging. To reiterate, get out there and take as many gigs as you can. This gets your name about as a player, and you get to meet other musicians. Eventually those musicians move on to shows or do deps for other people and will recommend you as a good player and a dep. You, of course, will have to have done a good job on the gigs that you did with them for them to recommend you, so make sure that every gig you do, no matter how small, is well prepared. You never know who you might meet at a gig.

Perseverance!

*"Many of life's failures are people who did not realise how close they were to success when they gave up." —
Thomas A. Edison*

Remember to keep your goal in sight and just go for it. As long as you believe in yourself and know that you have done the necessary preparation, you will get there. It will take time, and it can be tough at times, but as along as you get out there and play and get to know other musicians, your break will come. Just make sure that you are ready when it happens and

How to Get Work in Musical Theatre

prepare, prepare, prepare. As long as you have perseverance and passion for what you do, it will happen — just don't give up!

3

The Big Break

Your big break into theatre can come in a few different ways. As we discussed, it's likely to be as a deputy/substitute or if you are lucky enough to have been offered your first show contract. Let's have a look at this in more detail.

Depping/Subbing

Depping is the most common way to get into the theatre circles and to build your reputation as a player. (I will now use the term dep and depping for the rest of this chapter.) Some musicians do nothing but dep and cover on numerous shows. This gives them more variety over playing the same show eight times a week, and if one show closes they still have many others to fall back on, guaranteeing them work for the long run. These players also become known as reliable deps and get called on for other session work and last-minute emergencies. Some musicians have their regular show and still dep on other shows or functions just to get some variety.

I think that majority of theatre musicians have had to dep at some time. As we already discussed, in theatre it's all about your reputation and word-of-mouth recommendations. If a musician asks you in to dep on their show, they will need to feel confident that you are up to the job and that you can cope with the pressure. The MD will need to be assured that you can do the job and that the show won't be compromised. When a dep is booked, they have to be approved by the MD and the fixer, because if the show grinds to a halt because of a mistake from a dep, the MD and fixer will have to answer for it. In addition, the person who put the dep in will look bad in the eyes of the MD and fixer for having recommended someone substandard. As for the dep themselves — well, you're only as good as your last gig...

Doing Your First Dep

Doing a dep is not easy and can be the most stressful experience you will ever encounter. It's literally like jumping in at the deep end, since there is no rehearsal, and you will most likely do your first performance in front of a full audience. Although some of the regular musicians will do their best to help you get through it, there is often very little they can do to help. If you're the drummer, you are in the driver's seat, and most of the band will be listening to you and following you (you would like to hope so, anyway). Your best friends are the bass player and the MD, so watch and listen to them closely, but they will also expect you to know the show inside out, so don't rely on them entirely to get you through. You need to have a certain amount of confidence and authority, so take the lead but remember to watch the MD and make sure you follow them above all else. As soon as the band members feel that you are in charge and confident, they will follow and give you respect, but at the same time, if they feel that you are not up to the job, you might not get much assistance.

Now let's assume that you've made the contacts, you have done the gigs, and you are ready to start depping. The bass player you worked with on that function gig few months back liked your playing and has recommended you as a dep. The regular player has spoken to the MD, who has spoken to the fixer, and they all trust the bass player's judgement. You get booked to do your first dep. Now what? Well, first of all you need the music, often referred to as the 'pad' or the 'book,' and an up-to-date recording of the show. Always make sure that the recording that you were given and the pad are up to date. Ask the questions: 'Have there been any changes made to the show since this recording was done?' You don't want any surprises. Sometimes you will get the pad and recording on your first sit-in, or sometimes the regular player will post it to you, or even have it online for you to access. You can also ask if you can do your own recording of the show when you sit in. You can do this by using a headphone splitter from the monitor mixer and record your headphone mix into a recording device. Next step is to sit in. In the US it's called to 'watch the book' or 'auditing.' For most shows you will be required to sit in at least once before you can play the show, although this rule can vary, and it's common to have to sit in at least twice.

Note

Each fixer/contractor will have their own local protocols with regards to deputies. If more than one sit-in is dictated, it is common practise to pay deps for their second and any subsequent sit-ins. However, the deps themselves can choose to sit in as many times as they like and cannot demand payment for those sit-ins. It's in the deputies' interest to sit in as many times as they see fit, so that they feel prepared for the show.

On some shows you will have to play your first show with the regular player sitting next to you, or for him or her to be in the building. This is referred to as a 'Babysit.' If that goes well, you'll be allowed to play the show again without the regular in the building. If you feel you need more than two sit-ins to learn the show, make sure you do that — you can sit in as often as you like. Make sure your first sit-in is in plenty of time before your first dep, at least a few weeks. If you had the pad before, make sure you study it carefully before your sit-in and read through it with the recording, making any notes you need. When you sit in, watch the MD carefully and figure out where their down beat is (See 'Working with an MD' chapter). Take note of any cues and mark on the pad if you get 1,2,3,4 or 3,4 count-ins, etc. You can even ask to video the MD. This can be a very useful tool, since you can practise following him or her in your practise room. I would recommend videoing the visual monitor of the MD, and not the MD directly.

Tip

As a dep you should try to emulate the regular player's playing as much as possible. This will make the other musicians feel more at ease and make the show sound more consistent. However, improving on the part and adding some of your personality is fine, as long as it's done musically and in context.

Take the pad home and learn it inside out. Drummers — check tempos and any tempo changes and write them down as a reference, especially if there is no click. Get the tempo changes into your body. You need to be able to watch the MD as well as play the show, so you don't want to have your head buried in the music. Play the show along to the recording until it feels comfortable. I would recommend playing the show through at least four to six times before your first dep. Eliminate any potential pitfalls like page turns and other logistical issues like swapping guitars and patch changes. Practise those while learning the music; this will make them a part of your muscle memory and should make the process smoother and mistakes less likely.

Tip

Patch changes and instrument changes can often be quick and in awkward places. Make sure you practise these well before your first show so that you know exactly when to press a certain pedal or swap guitars. Factor in the time these can take, including plugging in, and make sure that all your instruments are tuned in advance.

Mark your music with every detail. (Always mark the pad with a pencil and not a pen, since you might need to make changes.) Don't leave anything to chance; things you think you will remember you are likely to forget when performing live. It's a good idea to use colour to highlight important things like patch changes. I've known guitarists and keyboard players to use different coloured stickers to mark in patch changes and other important actions. Do whatever you have to do to make your life as easy as possible. Try and learn the start of the show by heart, since this is where you'll be the most nervous when you perform it for the first time. If you feel confident at the start, it will give you a little time to settle into the show and hopefully start to relax a little more. Do your second sit-in when you have learned the show reasonably well. Use this sit-in to double-check things and watch the MD carefully for any cues and count-ins.

The time has come: your first dep is tonight. You've learned the music so that you can pretty much play it from memory, and you feel ready. So here are some general tips to make the experience as smooth as possible.

- Arrive early.
- Wear appropriate and smart pit attire.

- When you're in the theatre, go and check the equipment. Is your seat comfortable and at the right height? Is everything working? Check your in-ears or headphones.

- Check the mix on your monitor mixer. Are the click and your instrument loud enough?

- Make sure the music is in order.

No matter what you do, you WILL be nervous. But that's okay; sometimes it's good to feel nervous. It means that your alertness will be up, but try to relax, since adrenaline can have an effect on your playing. If you suffer from nerves, be aware of the effect it has on your playing and try to combat it the best you can. Bear in mind that even if your first show goes well, it's often show two or three where things start to go wrong, since you start to relax. You often think, *Well, I've done my first show, everything went well so I can relax now.* Don't relax too much just yet. Stay alert for every show — treat every show like your first. Remember, your reputation is everything. Don't mess it up by being complacent or arrogant.

Being a deputy can sometimes feel like a thankless task. Don't expect to get much praise after doing a dep. Many of the players who do the show regularly will be out of that pit before you've even taken your headphones off, and others will be used to having deps in on a regular basis so will not pay too much attention to who is in for a particular show. Have a quick word with the MD after the show and ask if he or she has any notes for you. There is every chance that they will give you some notes and comments about your performance. This is totally normal and expected, so just make sure that you take them on board and implement them for your next performance.

THE NA: THE NEVER AGAIN

If you totally mess up your dep (and this goes for your first or your twenty-fifth dep), or if the MD just doesn't like what you do, they can either give you notes to try to fix the issues, or they can give you the NA. This basically means that you will never be allowed to play that show again, at least while the current MD is in charge. You might not get this news directly from the MD; the regular player might have to tell you the bad news, or you might just never get asked again to dep on that show. This may sound rather harsh and cut-throat, but this is unfortunately how it works. Some MDs are more tolerant than others and will give deps more chances than some to get it right, while others are extremely particular about what they want and will give NAs after just one show. This is why preparation is so crucial, and to try and imitate as much as possible what the player that you are depping for does, since this is what the MD is used to hearing and is happy with. By doing the preparation, you can minimise the likelihood of getting the NA, and it's something that you want to try to avoid. However, as mentioned, some MDs are very particular, so you could get the NA even if you did a good job. If that happens, don't let it totally ruin your self-confidence. Look at what could have caused the issues and then learn from your experience and mistakes. Pick yourself up and move on; it's all a part of the show musician's learning curve.

How Do You Become the Regular Player on a Show?

After doing numerous deps on different shows and building up your reputation as a good and reliable player, your turn will come to get your own show. The way this happens can vary and is often from being in the right place at the right time, from knowing the right people, from a good reputation, or a combination of all these. Sometimes the regular player on a show that you've been depping on decides to leave to do another show, and you step into their seat, or you did a great job on a show and the fixer decides to offer you a show because of great recommendations from the other band members. You could also be friends with an MD who requests to have you in the band. However it happens, just make sure that you do the same diligent preparation for the show as you've done for the deps you've done. Just because you've landed your own contract, it doesn't mean you can't get sacked.

Your First Show as the Contracted Player

If you are the contracted player, the advice is similar to being a dep. The major difference is that you will most likely have some band rehearsals prior to the first performance. However, the first band call is also a high-pressure moment, with the added disadvantage that you won't have been able to sit in and see the show prior to the first rehearsal. (This is discussed more in Chapter 8.) You will hopefully have been

The Big Break

sent the music in advance and a recording of the show, but this cannot always be guaranteed. If you do have the music in advance, the same amount of preparation is advised as if you were a dep. Try to find out as much as you can about the show, including any previous recordings that may be available, if it's an established show. This is recommended, regardless of whether you have been sent the pad or not.

Whether you're depping or the regular, playing live as opposed to playing in your practise room can often highlight unexpected issues in the music and your playing. It can take a few times playing through a show before these get ironed out. This can be anything from a difficult page turn to a cue from the conductor that is a little more awkward than you thought. Expect to have to play the show a number of times before you feel totally comfortable. For deps this can be an issue, since you might have a number of weeks between playing a show. Try to mark in the music any issues you find each time you play the show so you can remember them for next time.

This may all sound like a daunting experience, and in many ways it is, but when you do get your first show on your own merits, it's very gratifying. Also, being recognised as a player in the theatre circles is a rewarding experience. There are a fair number of musicians who work in theatre, but soon you realise that the circle is actually quite small and that most people know each other, or have at least heard of other players on the circuit. Hence, it's so important to always do a good job. People will always remember someone who messes up or does a substandard job. Doing a good job is in many ways just expected. There are many players out there ready to step in if you mess up, so remember to prepare, be a nice person, get on with people, and you will get there. Despite the often potentially stressful environment, being a show musician can be a lot of fun, and you are often playing with some great musicians, so try to enjoy the moment

4

Working in Musical Theatre

After everything we have talked about in the previous chapters — all these years of hard work, preparation, and networking — is it all really worth it, and what is it truly like working full-time in musical theatre? I suppose that depends on the individual and on many different factors. Have you always wanted to play musicals, or did you want to become a rich and famous rock musician? What inspired you to start playing your instrument in the first place and the music you love playing will have big say in how much you will enjoy musical theatre. This profession is unlikely to make you rich or famous, but in the majority of cases it can be a rewarding and an enjoyable career and can provide you with a good income for playing your instrument every day. What could be better than playing your instrument six days a week with a great bunch of musicians and getting paid well for it? Sounds amazing, and in most cases it is, but as in any profession, it's not always what you expected, and personal experiences can vary greatly. As freelance musicians we will frequently move from show to show, often working with a new bunch of musicians every time and playing different styles of music. How much you enjoy the show experience will often come down to the show you are playing at the time and the people involved. Some shows will be a great experience, musically and socially, while others will not. The reasons are mixed and often personal. For instance, you might not particularly enjoy a show musically, either because the musical style is not your favourite, or it is badly arranged. Or you could not enjoy a show because of social issues with some of your band members. Whatever it might be, you must remember that you are there as a professional, and you need to get on with the job and do the best you can, regardless.

What can also happen if you're on a long-running show is that the monotony can start to get to you, and boredom may kick in. As in many professions where you are doing very repetitive things for a long time, this is inevitable. A big part of being a show musician is dealing with all these scenarios in a professional manner and playing every show as well as you possibly can, regardless of mood, boredom, or other outside factors. If things start to bring you down, then just think, *I could be working in an office!* All of a sudden, things don't seem so bad. I will go into some of those factors in more detail and try and give you some advice on how to deal with certain scenarios that could arise while working as a professional show musician.

The Music in Musical Theatre

The music you are into and enjoy playing can have a big influence on how much musical gratification you get from a particular show. There can potentially be many different issues that affect the musical experience; sometimes it's obvious, and sometimes it just isn't. It can be as simple as a monitoring issue where some of the players can't hear some of the band properly, or there could be some discrepancies in the written music causing an issue. However, sometimes the issues are more deep-rooted and can be difficult to resolve. On occasion, the bands that get put together for a show aren't always the perfect combination of players. The musical supervisors and fixers can get it wrong and put together a bunch of musicians that just don't work well together as a band, and this can lead to an unmusical experience. It often only needs one band member to throw off the whole balance.

So if you are in a band where there are issues, how do you deal with it and improve things?

- Try to figure out what the issue is. It could even be you.

- Have a chat with other band members to see if they are also having any issues.

- Have a quiet word with the MD to find out their opinion on the matter.

- Remember to be super-sensitive in how you mention any issues. You don't want to insult anyone's playing ability.

- Remember that it's not your responsibility to fix issues. Always go to the MD first. He or she is responsible for the band and for giving any notes to the players.

The Show Musician

All being well, there are no issues in the band and it all sounds good. Great! Unfortunately, sometimes that is not enough. Musical theatre is very unique in the way that it is put together, and sometimes the music takes a back seat behind, well, pretty much everything else. Sounds a bit strange, I know, but the people in charge of what happens on stage are often more concerned with how it looks and the pace of the show than how stylistically correct or groovy the music is. So, often you'll find that tempos are set at a place for a particular song where it just doesn't feel right, only because it works for the choreography onstage. Or that great groovy section of a song needs to be played down super quietly because of dialogue that's happening on stage. Sometimes decisions are made that don't seem very musical or logical, but you have to play what is asked of you for every show, and this can be frustrating. There are so many aspects of a theatre production that you may not be aware of, which can affect musical decisions and you may find bizarre. You must try to see the productions as a whole — the music is just one element of a much bigger picture.

The work you take on as a show musician will vary in quality of music and musicians — some will be great, while others not so much. You will need to learn how to cope with both and how to make the most out of every situation. Just remember always to do the best job you can and be professional all the way.

The Repetition

When you've been playing the same show for a number of weeks or months, the notes will be so instilled in your body that you will be able to play the entire show without much direct concentration. This is often referred to as muscle memory or autopilot and is when you have repeated a motion so many times that your body can emulate that motion without you thinking about it. This can be a comfortable place, since you feel totally relaxed and at ease with the music, but it can also be very dangerous. Your mind can start to wander, and you start thinking about everyday things. Because your body is on autopilot, if anything unexpected happens, it can really throw you, and mistakes can happen. So try to be aware of this happening and stay alert throughout the show. You need to be able to deal with the unexpected, like clicks failing, things going wrong on stage, and deps on other instruments.

When there's a dep on another instrument, make sure that you are on your guard. Count those bars that you normally feel your way through. Don't rely on those little figures from the keys that alert you about the next section coming up. The dep might not play them or might play something slightly different. Don't be caught out, since you will most likely look like the fool — not the dep.

To avoid falling into the autopilot trap, you can do things to get yourself motivated and more alert before a show. It's all about getting yourself into the right frame of mind. Find things that will inspire you to play before the show. Listen to some music that you enjoy and that makes you want to play — whatever makes you feel more enthusiastic about playing your instrument. You can also find things in the show to improve on, so try to concentrate on that, getting every note perfect, for example. You can also try changing your monitor mix slightly, turn up one of your fellow musicians and listen to what they are playing; this can often inspire you to play better or in a slightly different way. Find different ways to inspire you. This will help with the inevitable monotony of playing the same thing eight times a week.

THE DIFFERENT TYPES OF SHOWS IN MUSICAL THEATRE

Although they are all referred to as 'musicals,' shows do vary in how they are structured. Let's have look at some of the variations.

The Traditional Musical

These are shows written specifically as musicals where the story gets told directly in the lyrics of the songs. Some of these have very little actual dialogue, since almost everything is sung. The music can vary, from more of a classical format with orchestral arrangements to others that can be more contemporary, with a rhythm section and more of a rock sound. Some of these shows have been made into movies, but most started out as stage musicals. Examples of shows in this format are:

- Most of Andrew Lloyd Webber's shows, including *Phantom of the Opera*, *Jesus Christ Superstar*, *Cats*, and *Evita*
- *Miss Saigon*
- *West Side Story*

- *Les Misérables*
- *Hairspray*
- *Wicked*

The Jukebox Musical

These are shows where popular songs were adapted into a musical. The story does, to an extent, get told through the lyrics in the music but was usually not composed for that purpose; it was adapted to fit the story of the musical. This type of musical is gaining in popularity, probably since the music is already well known and is therefore easier to market to the general public. Examples of this type of show are:

- *Mamma Mia!*
- *Jersey Boys*
- *Rock of Ages*
- *We Will Rock You*
- *The Buddy Holly Story*

Film Musicals

These are musicals that started out as movies and were then adapted for the stage. Some of these can also be classed as Jukebox Musicals. These include:

- *Footloose*
- *Pricilla Queen of the Desert*
- *Legally Blonde*

- *High School Musical*

There are also the sorts of hybrid shows where an idea was taken from a famous movie or book and then original music written to tell the story. These would include:

- *Billy Elliott*
- *Charlie and the Chocolate Factory*
- *Shrek*
- *Spamalot*

These are just a few examples, and there are of course many more musicals out there. Make sure you do some research and check some of them out. It is good to have some knowledge of the popular musicals if you are planning on making this your career.

DEFINITION OF A WEST END AND A BROADWAY THEATRE

The terms West End and Broadway have now become the hallmarks of the theatre world. This is where thousands of tourists flock to see the latest blockbuster musical, as well as plays and other theatrical productions. The terms essentially refer to a theatre's location within the theatre hub of London or New York City.

The West End is an area in the west side of London's city centre, where many of the city's biggest theatres are located. However, the term now has more implications than mere location, since rates of pay are reflected in whether a theatre is an official West End theatre or not. To be an official West End theatre, it has to be a part of the Society of London Theatre, or SOLT. The theatres that are not members of SOLT are either not within the West End area or are smaller or non-commercial theatres and often are referred to as Fringe theatres or off-West End, which is a more recent term taken from the off-Broadway term.

Broadway is the name given to the theatre district in midtown Manhattan in New York City. Originally, whether or not a theatre was classed as a Broadway theatre was based on location alone, but is now based on the theatre's size and not just location. Theatres with a seating capacity of 100–499 are now classed as off-Broadway theatres, regardless of whether they are within the original Broadway hub. Theatres with 500 or more seats are classed as Broadway theatres and belong to the Broadway League. Theatres with less than 100 seats are classed as off-off-Broadway.

Show Performance Times

Show times do vary between shows and theatres, although they in general follow a similar pattern. What determines the time a show is put on is dependent on the type of show and the target audience. In the UK the typical show time format would be Monday to Saturday at 7:30 p.m. and then two matinees (daytime performance), one always on a Saturday at 2:30 p.m. and another on either a Wednesday or a Thursday at 2:30 p.m. On Broadway the show times are commonly at 7:00 p.m. Monday to Thursday and 7:30 or 8:00 p.m. on Fridays and Saturdays, with matinees usually being at 2:00 p.m. When a show is tailored more for adults, and where you can expect a more party atmosphere, the show times are sometimes changed so that there are no midweek matinees, but instead there will be two shows on a Friday at 5:00 p.m. and then 8:00 p.m. This is referred to as 'back-to-back shows' because of the small gap between them. There are some variations in this, which can be theatre-specific. For instance, some theatres prefer to have shows starting at 7:45 rather than 7:30, or even at 7:00 p.m. or earlier. On some children's shows there will also be a morning performance at 10:00 or 11:00 a.m., making the schedule rather hectic with three shows on a Saturday. This is particularly common on pantomime Christmas shows in the UK.

Sunday shows are becoming more and more common. On a show that has regular Sunday shows, Monday will most likely be your day off. The show schedule will therefore run from Tuesday to Sunday, with the get-in day (the show setup day) being a Tuesday, if it's a touring show. The bigger shows might even have a Wednesday get-in if extra time is needed to get the set into a theatre. This is covered in more details in the 'Touring' chapter. If a show lands on a Sunday, you may receive an extra Sunday payment. The Sunday fee does vary and is covered in more detail later in this chapter.

Theatre shows vary in length, but it is common that each act is about one hour, with a twenty-minute interval (intermission), making the overall show length about two and a half hours, give or take a few minutes. There are of course exceptions, and some shows are much longer and some shorter, although usually the producers will try to fit them within a three-hour call time so as to not go into overtime.

WHAT CAN I EXPECT TO GET PAID?

The monetary aspect of theatre varies greatly between shows and often between players, so it's difficult to give you exact figures. However, there are salary minimums set by the unions like The Musicians' Union in the UK and the American Federation of Musicians in the States (AFM), but you will need to be on a union-agreed contract to guarantee getting the minimum. Fortunately, when booked to play the big production shows, either in the West End of London on Broadway, or the big touring shows, you will in many cases be paid above the minimum set by the unions, depending on the show. There are also other extra payments that you may get on top of your basic, which I'll get into in a little while.

I won't be able to cover every single payment and contractual detail in this book. There are just too many clauses and different contracts that have many variants of pay. There is the West End, Broadway, and the different touring contracts, as well as separate agreements with independent theatres, etc. There are also two separate rates for productions that do eight shows a week and shows that do twelve shows a week — plus the rates can change on a yearly basis as new terms and rates are negotiated. To cover every detail and variation would be enough to fill another book. I will therefore only touch on what I feel are the most common elements you are likely to encounter, although this will depend on the work you ultimately end up doing. More details can always be found on your union website if you want to look into this further.

Note

Although the figures displayed in this section are in most part accurate as of the time of writing (2016–17), they are only to give you a general idea and should not be used as a reference.

The West End

A West End show will usually follow the SOLT agreement, which stands for Society of London Theatres. The performance rates are renegotiated frequently, but at the time of writing the weekly rate for a musician is in the region of £1,000. This is normally based on an eight-show week, so any extra calls, performances, or rehearsals would be paid on top. You would then possibly get additions on top, like doubling or trebling, porterage, and holiday pay, which I'll go into later. Musical directors and assistant musical directors will also get a slightly higher rate than other musicians because of the extra hours and responsibilities. The MD or conductor is the highest paid person in the orchestra, followed by the assistant MD. MDs will often negotiate their fee depending on their experience.

If you are performing a show in what is referred to as a 'small theatre' in the West End, the small theatre agreement will be used. This lowers the minimum salary paid to musicians to three quarters of the normal SOLT agreement minimum for theatres of 799 seats or less; this would include the theatres Apollo, Garrick, Harold Pinter, Wyndhams, and Playhouse. For theatres of 700 seats or less, two thirds of the minimum would be paid. In addition, the MU has separate agreements with some of the better-known theatres and theatre companies, including the Royal Shakespeare Company, the Royal National Theatre, and Menier Chocolate Factory. See the MU website for more details on those: www.musiciansunion.org.uk

Broadway

Broadway musicians follow the Local802 contract — the Broadway Collective Bargaining Agreement, CBA — which at the time of writing is around $1,700 a week basic, again based on an eight-show week. You then get other additions on top, including doubling, onstage payment, media fee, vacation, and instrument maintenance fees. The conductor gets a higher rate, which can be in the region of $3,700 a week. For your average musician, you will probably be looking at about $2,000–$2,400 a week, and the associate conductor on about $2,800 a week. See below for other extras.

The smaller theatres in New York City are often referred to as off-Broadway or off-off-Broadway, as explained earlier. The AFM has separate agreements with some of these theatres, similar to the MU in the UK. These agreements guarantee a minimum rate for musicians, which is lower than the Broadway CBA. See www.local802afm.org for more information.

Fringe Theatre

Some fringe or independent theatres will use separate agreements that have not been approved by the unions (see non-union agreements below) and will therefore pay less than the union minimums. Some independent theatres will only pay enough to cover expenses and not much else. This is something you could consider to gain experience, but I would not normally advise taking on shows for little money, since it just encourages the producers to pay less, and it's clearly not enough to earn a living. In these difficult times for musicians, we need to try to stand together against pay cuts and exploitation. Seek advice from your local union before you sign any contract that you are not totally happy with or don't understand.

Non-Union Agreements

A non-union agreement is as the name suggests, an agreement that is not approved by the musicians' union. The terms that the union set in regards to pay and working conditions are often not followed in these contracts, so think carefully before you sign a contract that does not have union backing. If you do decide to accept a non-union agreement, make sure that you read it very carefully, and make sure you understand every detail. Contracts are often written in a complex and confusing way and can be difficult to understand. This can be done on purpose to try to disguise the more subtle parts of the contract, which could potentially have a big impact on you as the contractee. Make sure you ask for clarification about anything that you are unsure about, and if there are elements in the contract that you are not happy with, consider either getting professional help, negotiate better terms if possible, or don't accept the contract.

I always recommend using a union-approved contract. You can then get free professional advice and clarification on the terms within the contract. Also, if you have any issues during the term of your contract, the unions will be there to help and advise you. This of course only applies if you are a union member. Remember that many of the benefits and rules that the unions have fought hard to get implemented for musicians will most likely not apply if you sign a non-union contract. General employment law should still stand, but minimum rates of pay set by the unions do not have to be honoured.

Tip

If you decide to try to negotiate better terms for your offered contract, regardless of whether it's a union or non-union contract, make sure you do so in a sensible and courteous manner. Don't put forward an unreasonable request, and be prepared to give and take. Often the fixer or musical contractor have very little flexibility on the terms, so don't push too hard, since this could cost you the gig.

It's of course up to you if you sign a non-union contract, but just make sure that you look into it carefully and make sure that you are not being exploited. Remember that the unions are constantly trying to better the terms and rates for musicians, and the more musicians settle for lower-rate non-union contracts, the more it undermines the work of the union and potentially will lower the rates that musicians will be paid. At the end of the day it has to be your judgement.

Doubling

Doubling is when a musician plays more than one instrument on a show. For instance, guitarists are classed as doubling if they play an electric and an acoustic guitar. Woodwind players are usually classed as doubling if they play a tenor saxophone and a clarinet. If they also played a flute, for example, it would be classed as trebling. For both doubling and trebling there is an extra fee on top of your basic pay.

In the West End it's 15% on top of your weekly basic. If you play more than three instruments, you will get an additional 15% payment, but special permission is needed from the MU before this is agreed.

On UK touring shows that follow the UKT Agreement, doubling is now referred to as 'up to two instruments' and is included in the minimum. Trebling, or 'up to one additional instrument,' is 10% on top of doubling. Quadrupling, or four instruments, is 15% above trebling.

Note

In some instances the band all get paid the same fee, regardless of how many instruments you play. This fee would usually be above the union minimum and would include doubling and other extras that would normally be paid separately on top of the minimum. If you play numerous instruments and feel that the fee does not reflect this, you will have to negotiate any further payments. Seek advice from your union if in doubt.

On Broadway there is an increasing scale of up to ten instruments, which is paid on top of your base wage, ranging from 12.5% for one double to 68.75% for ten doubles.

On US Pamphlet B touring shows, doubling is 20% on top of minimum weekly salary for one double, 15% for 2nd double, and 8.5% for 3rd double and above. On the SET agreement it's 15% on top for one double, 10% for two, and 7% for three. No extra payment is made above three doubles. This is paid on top of your normal weekly basic salary. (I will explain the Pamphlet B and SET contracts in more detail later.) Check the local802afm.org for more details of the most recent fees.

Extra Calls

Extra calls are any calls that you do on top of your contracted eight calls a week. So for instance, if a rehearsal or an extra show gets scheduled in and you are still doing your normal eight shows that week, you will be paid an extra fee on top of your normal basic wage.

In the West End and on UK touring shows, you get paid 1/8th on top of your regular weekly fee, or one extra show fee. On Broadway you get paid time and a half on top. On US touring shows any extra performances are paid at 2/8ths of the player's weekly salary, as per the Pamphlet B contract. An extra call is a three-hour time slot, and if you go over the three hours you are into overtime.

Overtime

Overtime is paid if you exceed the allowed maximum weekly working hours, if you exceed a scheduled call time, or if you are required to work outside normal working hours. If you are on a show that is long and it goes over the three-hour call time, you will get paid overtime. This will also apply if the show happens to go up late or if there are any other delays that cause the call to exceed the three hours' call. The way overtime is calculated varies for different contacts, so let's have a look at some of these.

On the SOLT and the UKT Agreements, you get paid time and a half if your performance exceeds the agreed call time, usually three hours. This is computed in five-minute units on the SOLT agreement and in fifteen-minute units on the UKT. This is calculated to the nearest five- or fifteen-minute increments, so if you work three minutes overtime, you get paid for extra five minutes on the SOLT and extra fifteen minutes on the UKT. Similar rules apply to overtime in the US, but it's commonly calculated in half-hour increments.

Some contracts will have some allowances for extra duties already included in your fee. This is common for MDs who can have things like vocal warmups and possibly some rehearsals included in their salary. There are also some other clauses in the contracts discussed above with regards to rehearsals and production period overtime. I would encourage you to check out the relevant contract for more information on these at your local union website.

Breaks and Rest Days

In general, you are entitled to a fifteen-minute break in every three-hour call that you do, or five minutes in every hour — the interval in a show performance is classed as your break. There are some variations to this when it comes to rehearsals and extra calls, and you can check these out on your relevant contract. The MD and company manager should make sure that the breaks are scheduled in and are implemented during rehearsals and other calls that you do.

Porterage

Porterage is a payment made for you to transport your instrument to and from the venue. On stationary shows like in the West End and on Broadway, this will be paid in the first week and last week, or whenever you have to move your instrument from the theatre or regular place of work. On touring shows this will be paid weekly, if you have to take your instrument away each week, and it cannot be transported with the show. If flight cases are provided and your instrument is transported with the show between venues, portage will usually not be paid on a weekly basis.

In the West End, porterage ranges from £19.38 to £57.47 depending on instrument. On the UKT agreement, porterage ranges from £11.46 to £22.92.

On Broadway, if a large instrument needs to be transported prior to a first rehearsal or performance, a round-trip rate of up to $25 is paid. On Pamphlet B agreements in the US, a reimbursement of $15.60 for each journey is payable to the musicians if they have to transport their instruments themselves. Bulky instruments will always be transported by the show.

Sunday Performances

If you have performances on a Sunday, you could receive an extra payment, but this is dependent on the contract you're on. Some contracts also have extras for public holidays. Check your contract for this.

In the West End on the SOLT agreement, Sunday shows either entitle you to a day off in lieu or an extra payment of double time. On the UKT agreement, you will receive an extra payment on top of your basic of £54.65 for one Sunday show and £76.51 for two Sunday shows. (Correct as of time of writing.)

On Broadway there is no extra payment for a single Sunday performance, but an extra payment of time and a half is payable if a second Sunday show is performed. On US touring Pamphlet B agreements, there is also no dedicated Sunday show payment. Performances can land on any day of seven, as long as there is one day off a week.

Sound Checks and Setting-Up Fees

Sound checks are usually classed as an extra call and will not be classed as a part of your eight shows a week rate. Depending on the show, the sound check can range from a minimum of a one-hour call to a full three-hour call, but is commonly a three-hour call, including the setup time. If you have a lot of equipment that takes more than fifteen minutes to set up and/or strike down, for instance percussion or drums, then you may be eligible to get paid overtime or an extra setup call to cover the setup and packing-up time. Check with your manager (fixer/contractor) about this.

Note

In the UK, you are expected to be ready to play ten minutes before the start of the show. Regardless of the contract, you will always be expected to be ready to play at 'beginners,' which is five minutes before curtain up.

On UK touring shows, a 'short call' rate can be used for sound check and rehearsal, as per the UKT agreement. A 'short call' is a maximum of two hours. Some contracts have the sound check and setup as a part of a one-off weekly rate, including the eight shows. If this is case, make sure you check your contract for the full details so that you are not being paid below the minimum rate. A seating call of up to thirty minutes before a rehearsal or a sound check can be a part of your contract and does not incur extra payment. Check your contract for this.

On US touring shows, a sound check is paid as a one-hour minimum call and then in half-hour increments after that.

Whatever your contract states, make sure you understand what the deal is, since you will have a hard time questioning any terms after you've signed the contract. Contact the union for advice with any possible issues.

Onstage Payments

If you're on the SOLT agreement in the West End, you should get an extra payment if you are onstage while playing. This is a small extra payment for each performance, and there is also an extra fee for additional costume. On UK touring shows that use the UKT agreement, onstage payment is part of the minimum rate, and no extra is paid.

In the US on Broadway under the CBA agreement and the Pamphlet B touring agreement, an extra payment is made if a musician has to perform onstage or move from the pit to the stage or another part of the theatre during a performance.

Make sure that you check your role carefully, if you are an onstage musician, and that you are happy with any extras you may need to do. Check the union for the up-to-date rates, and be aware of the extras you should potentially get. If you are on a flat rate, make sure that any extra duties are reflected in the fee.

Holiday/Vacation Pay

You are entitled to holiday pay, which is calculated as percentage of the hours worked. You accumulate these holiday credits, which you can then either take as official holiday off the show and put a dep/sub in to cover, or you get them paid on top of your salary at set intervals, usually every twelve weeks or at the end of the contract. On many touring shows in the UK, there will be gaps in the touring

Working in Musical Theatre

schedule, and these will then be classed as holiday weeks, and you will be paid your basic pay (so no touring allowance or travel, etc.). The producers can schedule up to four weeks holiday in a twelve-month contract. The holiday pay on UK touring shows is calculated as 1/12th of your basic salary per week, which means that every twelve weeks you will have accrued one week's holiday.

In the States, it's referred to as Vacation Pay. On Broadway it's included in your weekly salary and is calculated as 6.125% of your basic. On Pamphlet B productions, no vacation pay is payable for productions of less than four weeks. For five weeks or more, 3.5% off the minimum is payable. After six months cumulative service, you are entitled to one week's vacation. You need to give a minimum of thirty days notice and are requested to try to take your vacation in a large city where a cover is more easily available. If on a foreign tour, no vacation is allowed, and the accrued money will be credited.

This may all sound very complex and difficult to work out, but this should all be worked out for you and paid into your bank account by the producers or their representative. Please remember that union rates and terms are altered and renegotiated on a regular basis, so make sure that you check your local union website for the most up-to-date rates. I would also encourage you to read the relevant agreement before you sign to get a more in-depth understanding of the many different elements that make up the contract. For Broadway go to www.local802afm.org and for the MU in the UK go to www.musiciansunion.org.uk

UK Touring Shows

In the UK, the UKT agreement is normally used, which is, like the SOLT agreement, negotiated by the Musicians Union' with the theatre producers. UKT stands for United Kingdom Theatre. I have already covered some of the extras, like doubling and overtime, but I will now cover the more touring-specific elements. Unlike the SOLT agreement, there is no small-theatre rate for the UKT agreement, but there are two rates of pay, one for the commercial sector and the other for the subsidised sector. There are a number of theatres in the UK that are subsidised by national arts councils and local governments, where a lower rate of pay has been negotiated. So as to not overcomplicate things, I will only include figures for the commercial sector in this book. Please check the UKT agreement for further information.

At the time of writing, the UKT minimum for an eight-show week is £588.13 for the commercial sector. However, when touring there are a few extras paid on top as standard.

Touring Allowance

Touring allowance is also set by the UKT and is paid to cover accommodation on tour and living expenses. At the time of writing, it is £240 a week. Touring allowance is not paid if your home address is within twenty-five miles of the venue you are playing. This is normally worked out using mapping software like Google Maps, the AA route planner or similar, using the shortest route.

Travel

Travel expenses are paid on top of your basic and are calculated from your home address to the first venue on the tour, and then from venue to venue. When a week off is scheduled in the touring schedule, you will be paid to your home address and then back to the next venue on the tour. You are not paid to go home on your one day off a week.

You will usually get the option at the start of the tour to choose for your travel expenses to be calculated either using mileage, which at the time of writing is £0.26 a mile, or as a second-class rail fare. You will then have to stick to that decision, and you cannot swap from mileage to rail fare, or vice versa, halfway through the tour.

US TOURING SHOWS

Touring in the US is a little more complex, since there are rules in place for each union local or state to protect the local musicians and performers. An agreement has to be reached prior to the production arriving in each locale to determine how many local musicians will be used in the production. Only certain pre-arranged personnel are allowed to perform in a local outside their own. See the 'Touring' chapter for more information.

Touring shows in the States essentially follow two different agreements, the Pamphlet B Agreement and the SET Agreement (sometimes referred to as the SETA).

Most of the bigger productions in the US follow the Pamphlet B agreement. These are shows that will typically stay for more than a week in each town. At the time of writing the weekly minimum salary is $1,293.65 for musicians, $1,617.04 for assistant conductors, and $2,005.18 for conductors.

The Pamphlet B Agreement also includes the SET (Short Engagement Tour) agreement, which covers touring productions that stay in each town for a week or less. There are some exceptions to this, for instance if the production is touring under the Actors Equity Full Production Agreement; then the full Pamphlet B Agreement is used and not the SET. The SET agreement allows lower rates than the Pamphlet B on salaries and other rates. The weekly minimum salary for SETA is $900 for musicians, $1,125 for assistant conductors, and $1,395 for conductors. Check the union website for up-to-date information at www.afm.org.

Out-of-Town Living Expenses in the US

Just as in the UK, performers also are paid living expenses for being away from home. This varies slightly depending on which city you're working in. For all Pamphlet B engagements in San Francisco and New York, and for engagements of less than four weeks in Boston, Chicago, Los Angeles, Philadelphia, Toronto, and Washington, D.C., the weekly rate is $938 or $134 a day, seven days a week. For all other towns it's $896 a week or $128 a day (again correct at the time of writing). If you are provided with some meals and accommodation by the employer, the weekly rate could be lower, but this will be agreed upon prior to the engagement starting.

The SET agreement rate is lower. The amount of your per diem is based upon where you stay, whether you choose producer-provided lodging, or find your own. If the musician elects not to accept provided housing from the producer and chooses to find their own lodging, the per diem is $86 a week; otherwise it is $50 for a single occupancy and $68 for double occupancy. All accommodation provided must be of an AAA, double-diamond standard or better.

OTHER RELEVANT INFORMATION

Sick Pay

As musicians we are entitled to sick pay as per general employment law. This will of course vary greatly between countries, but in general you should be eligible for sick pay at your full rate of pay for a certain amount of days. This will then revert to statutory sick pay as set by the government guidelines. Depending on how long you are off work, at a certain point your employer will most likely be able to legally stop paying you, as per general employment laws. You will of course need to have an official doctor's note, which signs you off work, for this to be implemented. You will most likely need to arrange your own cover, even for medical or sick leave, so make sure that you have some deputies prepared as soon as possible at the start of a new show. Check your contract and government websites for more accurate information on sick pay.

Terminating a Contract

If you want to terminate your contract before the agreed contract end date, you can give notice to the producer. You would do this in writing and send it to your representative, which in most cases would be the fixer/musical contractor.

The notice you need to give varies depending on the contract signed but ranges from two weeks to a couple of months. I would always recommend giving as much notice as possible and try to have a replacement lined up. This could potentially be one of your regular deps who already knows the show. Terminating your contract early is sometimes not looked on favourably and can potentially jeopardise future employment with the relevant fixer, so make sure you only do this for a good reason and try to make the process as easy as possible.

The producers can also terminate your contract early, for various reasons. The show could not be selling particularly well, so they might want to cut their losses, or the producers could go bust and the show gets pulled. The notice period they need to give you as the musicians will be in your contract and is usually the same as your notice period. It's worth bearing in mind that even if you've signed a year's contract, this may be terminated before the contract end date.

Taxes

Tax liability is one of those subjects that most of us hate. It's never great to have to hand over a substantial amount of your hard-earned money to the taxman, but it's something that is unavoidable and necessary. As self-employed musicians it's something that we need to be aware of and unfortunately need to organise for ourselves. Make sure that you put money aside for your tax bill every paycheque and that you are organised right from the start with your tax. Make sure you know when your tax bill has to be submitted to the Inland Revenue in the UK, the Internal Revenue Service (IRS) in the US, or whatever the tax authority is in your country or region.

I go into tax in more detail in the self-employment chapter of this book, so check that out for more information.

Pension

Pensions are another subject that we often forget to think about. Although there are some state pensions available to most of us (if you have been paying your tax, as you should), most of us are now aware that there is a chance there won't be much pension available when we eventually need it. Because we work as self-employed, we have to be responsible for organising our own pension scheme, at least to a degree. The musicians' unions do have a pension scheme in place now, in which you will be auto-enrolled while you're working, but since there are often gaps in our employment, you may want to think about a secondary pension option. The options for pensions are always changing, so look carefully into what is the best option for you wherever you live, but the most important thing is to get some plan into action so that you don't get stung later on in life.

Make sure that you check out any pension providers very carefully and what guarantees you will have of getting your money back when you eventually need it. You could also look into other ways of investing your money, whether it's in property or stock. I am no financial expert, so can't really advise or recommend any particular provider or option, but I just want to make you aware that it's something you need to think about. You can also get advice from your musicians' union about pension-related issues.

Insurance

Make sure that your instrument is insured, and insured well enough that you can replace it with the same or better if it is damaged beyond repair or is stolen. Don't neglect this, since you must remember that if you are working as a musician, and you don't have a working instrument, you don't work and don't get paid, so it's a worthwhile investment. On touring shows your instruments will usually be insured by the producers while in transit and in the theatres, but they will not be insured while in your possession on the way to the first venue, for example. Therefore, I still advise having your own insurance, just in case.

Also, make sure that you have personal liability insurance. What is that? If you are working as a musician and someone is injured because of your instrument or actions, they could potentially sue you for damages. In today's 'sue everybody' society, it is worth covering any such scenarios, even though they are potentially unlikely. Luckily, if you are a member of the musicians' union, you will automatically be covered by public liability insurance up to ten million pounds. The UK musicians' union also offers complimentary £2,000 instrumental insurance, and you have the option of increasing that for an extra yearly fee. There are also other benefits on offer, like personal accident cover and personal expenses cover, which helps with the cost of dealing with tax authorities. In the US, the AFM also includes public liability insurance in their membership, and you have the option of getting a discounted insurance for your instrument, so make sure you utilise those offers. Your union fee is worth it just for those two perks alone.

TAKING TIME OFF

There will come a time when you will need to take time off your show. This could be for family reasons, medical reasons, holiday, or to do other gigs. Having time off is healthy thing, especially on a long-running show, so make sure you do allow yourself some time off and a chance to do other things. This is good for your mental state and for your ability as a musician, since playing the same thing eight times a week can take a toll in many ways. When it's time to request some time off, it's crucial to do it in the right way, that all the relevant people are informed, and that your part is properly covered. Unlike the cast, who have people to cover them on hand with swings and understudies, we musicians have to bring someone in, make sure they learn the show properly, and then trust that they turn up when they are supposed to.

The Protocol for Requesting Time Off

The process for taking time off can vary between shows and fixers, but the general protocol is the same. First of all, check with the MD if they are okay with you taking time off and who you are looking to have dep for you. Make sure you do this with plenty of notice. If the MD is okay with it, you need to contact the fixer/contractor, or the deputy supervisor/house contractor, depending on the local rules in place. I find that email is usually best, since that will make the request in writing and limits any issues down the line, especially if you are making the request a long time in advance. You will then always have written proof of any conversation, in case of any disputes or if there are double-bookings in the band.

Note

On Broadway it is common that each regular (the musician who is contracted to play the show) is required to name a maximum of five substitutes to come and learn the show.

Sometimes a dep book is used, where you can check if someone else has requested time off at the same time as you. If this is in place, it will often be stored in the pit, so check that first, since that can save you time before contacting the fixer and arranging a possible dep. For example, if you are the drummer and are requesting time off, and you are putting in a dep who is doing the show for the first time, and you then see that the bass player is taking that same show off, also with a new dep, you can be pretty certain you will not be allowed the time off. This is the case because it is not usually allowed for two key members of the same section to be off at the same time, especially if a new dep is being introduced.

There can be numerous rules in place with regards to taking time off on a show.

The most common ones are:

- No more than one member of a section can be off at the same time, rhythm section or brass section, etc. However, if one of the players is using a dep that has done the show a number of times, and the MD is comfortable with him or her, sometimes an exception is made.

- No more than one new dep is allowed at any one time in the band. For example, if a keys player puts in a dep for the first time, no one else can put a dep in that hasn't played the show before.
- You are not allowed to take time off to dep another show that has the same fixer. This rule is normally fixer-specific and not an across-the-board rule.

Other things to bear in mind when requesting time off are:

- When requesting time off, make sure that you ask, and don't demand it.
- Make sure that you request any time off with plenty of notice, at least a couple of weeks.
- Be polite at all times and respect the decisions of the MD and the fixer.
- Make sure that you put in a suitable dep for the show. Someone you trust to do a good job and that the MD and fixer have both approved.
- Never take time off without asking all the people involved. It can reflect extremely badly on you if you put in a dep that has not been approved, and they then make mistakes that compromise the show. Don't think that if you put a dep in without approval, it will just be okay. Follow the correct procedure.

How to Put a Dep In

So now you know how to request time off, but how do you find a suitable dep, and what do you need to do to make sure that they are ready? Some of these questions were answered earlier in the book in 'The Dep/Sub' section, but I will go through some of the most important things to bear in mind when booking a dep.

Step 1: Speak to the MD

What I usually do when booking a dep is ask the MD first who they would prefer to come in. There are numerous reasons for this. First of all, the MD is the one who will feel the change the most in the band when a new member comes in. With a new player in the band, the MD can expect that things may be slightly different and will possibly need to give even clearer cues than usual. They will have to be on high alert so that they can react quickly in case things go wrong. The MD needs to approve whoever comes in, so by asking the MD first, I am in essence covering two things at once. I am making the MD feel at ease that they will feel comfortable with whoever is coming in and trust them to do the job well, and I am getting the initial confirmation that I can book the time off.

Step 2: Check availability of dep/sub

The next stage is to contact the person the MD suggested. On some occasions the MD will have no preference about who comes in, so I will make some suggestions. It can be a good idea to have contacted a couple of possible deps beforehand to check their availability. You can then say, "So and so are available, how do you feel about them?" If there has been a prior production of the show you are doing, it can be worth checking who played or depped on it previously. The fixer will most likely know that, if it's the same fixer as before, or you can ask around to find out. As soon as you have names of two or more potentials, contact them, if you haven't already, and check their availability for the dates that you need. Be sure to tell them that this has not yet been confirmed and to just pencil in the dates until you confirm.

Step 3 Contact the fixer/musical contractor or the deputy supervisor/house contractor

Now you can email the relevant deputy organiser. If writing to the fixer directly, as is common in the UK, also put the name of the show and your instrument in the subject title, since some fixers deal with numerous shows, and it will make it clearer to them who they are dealing with. Use your own style, but the most important thing is to make sure that you ask if you can have the time off, and that you are polite. Some fixers deal with many musicians on many shows, and their main concern is that the show goes ahead for every performance to the same quality as when the regular players are on. If they feel there could be a compromise in the show, they have every right to refuse your request. So try not to give them any reason to think that there will be any issues, and cover your back through the entire process. By having all correspondence in writing, you can always show that things were agreed, in case there are any disputes or if there are any double-bookings in the band.

Preparing Your Dep/Sub

You've got a yes from all the relevant parties, so you can now confirm the dates with the dep that has been pencilled in. As explained in the 'Dep/Sub' section, your dep will need to sit in once at an absolute minimum, although twice is often standard (check the relevant local rules for this). Even if they have done the show before, if it's not this exact production, they will still need to sit in so that they can make notes of any little changes that will have been made to refresh their memory and to see how another MD conducts the show.

Note

In the UK, at least, if a dep is booked to cover an official holiday, a medical absence, or any other reason where a musician needs to take time off that is requested by the producers (for instance, where a dep is booked to cover the assistant MD while the MD does an official show watch), the company will pay for any sit-ins over the standard one, and they will also pay the dep directly for any performances they cover.

Now you need to send the dep the pad and a recording of the show to learn. I will normally scan in the music after I've marked it up with any notes, and then email the dep the pad as a pdf. I will do a recording of the show through my monitoring equipment, making sure that the dep will hear all the instruments in the band and the click. I will then use a cloud-based service like Dropbox to get that to them.

> **Tip**
> Make sure that you mark up the music for your dep with as much information as possible. Include count ins, patch changes, dynamics, and anything else that they need to look out for. Remember to include any recent changes made.

The next step is the sit-in. Arrange a time for your dep to come in, and make sure that you inform the sound department in advance, and your MD. This is important so that your dep has his or her own monitoring to use, which the sound department will arrange, and that they have somewhere to sit near you in the pit. If other members of the band also have people sitting in on the same show, things can get very cramped in the pit, and there also won't be enough monitoring to go around for all, so check with your MD first. Make sure that your dep has enough light to see the music, since they will most likely want to make some notes, and that they can see the MD clearly. They will need to be able to see all the cues and count-ins that the MD is doing. Another thing to bear in mind is that your dep can see you playing, since they will need to see some of the nuances in page turns, what guitar you are picking up, how you swap to sticks from brushes, etc., depending on your instrument.

Note

On some shows there won't be any space for a dep to sit next to you while they sit in. This is common if the band is on stage or there is little room in the pit. The dep will then have to sit wherever they can; sometimes a special room is prepared especially for this, with a monitor of the MD and an audio monitor mixer. In this circumstance you have to make sure that you inform your dep of any potential issues they can't see.

After the first sit-in, arrange the second sit-in with your dep, and after they've done that, you're good to go. Some deps will want to sit in more than twice, which is fine, since you want them to be as prepared as possible. If your dep is using your equipment, make sure you don't forget to talk them through your setup. Mention any possible tricky bits that you discovered at the start and how you have dealt with them. If your dep needs to pack your equipment away after the show, also talk them through that process and where everything needs to go. Just make sure that your dep is as prepared as they can possibly be. What you don't want is to get a phone call after the first show that your dep does, when you are in your first day of your week's holiday, being asked to come back because your dep has totally wrecked the show!

I have come across some musicians who have this notion that if they book a dep who is not that great, they will look better for it when they come back, and that it somehow keeps their job secure. Some won't even dare take a show off in fear of being replaced. I personally think this is overly paranoid and can be counterproductive. First of all, you are in a contract, so you will not lose your job, even if the dep is better than you — it just doesn't work like that. And second, if your dep is not suitable for the show or not good enough to cope, it will reflect badly on you, since you booked them. The MD will not be very impressed, since they have had to pull the show through with a substandard player in the band, and it will in turn jeopardise your chances of taking time off in the future. So my advice is to make sure you put someone in that is more than capable of doing the job well, and prepare them as well as possible.

How to Pay a Dep

Your dep has covered the show for you, and all went well. You will now need to pay your dep, unless of course it was a company dep, as mentioned earlier. I believe in treating your deps well, and I always try to pay my deps as soon as possible. Work out what the money is and send them the amounts and request an invoice. You will need this for your accounts, since what you pay your deps is classed as a business expense. I will normally pay my deps using a bank transfer. It's both quicker, and there is a definite record of the money being sent and received, eliminating any possible issues.

Pay your deps fairly. Some musicians try to pay their deps the minimum that they can get away with, or even less than the going rate. I think this is not an acceptable way to do business. The dep has done you a service, and you need to pay them fairly. I always pay my deps exactly what I get paid, and never less. On top of that, if it's a touring show, I will always pay their travel costs and subsistence. So how do you work out what to pay your dep?

In the West End or on Broadway, it's usually assumed that your dep will live reasonably locally, so just the show rate is paid. On a typical eight-show week, you will just divide your weekly fee by eight, which gets you your show rate, and then multiply that by how many shows your dep did. Add on any extra calls your dep may have done, like rehearsals and overtime, and don't forget to include things like doubling fees and any other extras that you get on your instrument. If your dep lives out of town, you need to negotiate whether you will pay them any travel money.

Note

On Broadway it is common that any regular subs go on the payroll and are then paid directly by the manager or producers.

On touring shows things get a little more complex. In the UK, on top of your show fee you will also have touring allowance and travel expenses (see the 'Touring' chapter). So here you take your touring allowance money and divide it by the number of days you work and then multiply by the days your dep did. The travel gets worked out in the UK by mileage (at time of writing, travel is calculated at 26 pence per mile) or 2nd class rail fare. Get your dep's home address and use an online tool like Google Maps to work out the distance in miles from their home and to the theatre where they will be playing. Choose the shortest route and then multiply that by two, since it will be a return journey. Multiply that number by 0.26 (26 pence a mile) and you have your travel expenses. If your dep is using public transport like rail or flying, it's usually best to come to an agreement, since these can vary greatly depending on what they've booked. Use the mileage rate as guide and negotiate from there. Add up the three figures, show rate, touring allowance, and travel, and you have your final figure. If your dep is using your digs, you can negotiate the touring allowance figure accordingly.

Try to get at least two or three deps up and running on your show. There is every chance that your regular dep won't always be available when you need him or her, so have a few options. Make sure that you go through the same procedure with all of your deps, and remember to treat your deps well. They will find out quickly if you are underpaying or if you are a late payer, and word will spread quickly.

THE EPK: ELECTRONIC PRESS KIT

An EPK is a press kit that is used to promote a show. This may include a short video advert with highlights from the show, as well as other promotional material. The EPK is sent to relevant media companies to help advertise the show. An EPK recording is done at the beginning of a show's run, usually in the first week or two when the show is into the performance week, after rehearsals and technical rehearsals. The whole cast and band will usually be called in for an extra call to record the EPK, but sometimes it is recorded during an actual performance or a dress rehearsal.

How you get paid for an EPK does vary, depending on the production company and whether you're on a touring show or in the West End or Broadway. In the West End SOLT agreement, an extra call to do the recording will be paid, and then a monthly usage fee is paid to the musicians involved in the recording. At time of writing that fee is £26.30.

The UKT agreement states that a recording of up to ten minutes of completed edited footage, for the express purpose of promoting, publicizing, and advertising the production, can be done at the musician's normal place of work. A two-week notice needs to be given before any recording takes place. Hours worked by the musician in connection with such recording form a normal part of working hours.

In the States a media fee is paid as part of the weekly salary, which includes usage of between three to fifteen minutes of recorded footage, depending on where it is broadcast.

Some non-union contracts have the recording and use of an EPK written into the contract and state that a certain number of minutes of footage of your performance can be used without any extra payment. Although if an extra call is needed to record the EPK, that will usually be an extra pay, unless otherwise stated in your contract.

Check your contract for the details of the EPK, or any press recording, so that you are aware of the procedure at the start of the contract period. Some contracts will have clauses about 'show promotion' or similar written in. These are more common for the cast, but look at this carefully to avoid any misunderstanding. Any issues will need to be addressed before the contract is signed. Check with your local union for more information.

THE SHOW REPORT

The stage management team is responsible for creating the 'Show Report.' This is a report that is created at the end of each and every show, listing any issues that may have occurred during the performance. Anything gets noted, from missed lines by the cast to show stops — basically anything that has had an impact on the normal running of the show. The Show Report is then emailed out to all the creative team and producers for them to analyse to see if there are any recurring issues with the show. Anyone involved in the show can make it into the show report, including musicians. If you made a mistake that would have had an impact on the show and was noticed by the stage management or creatives, your name would go in the report. Depending on the reason, this doesn't necessarily have any major consequences, but try to avoid this happening by staying consistent and professional, as discussed earlier.

5

Working in a Pit Environment

What exactly is a pit? It doesn't sound very inviting or glamorous, and in many cases it isn't. The pit environment can be an unnatural and often unmusical place to play.

In the old Victorian theatres in the UK and the older theatres on Broadway, the pits can be very small and inhospitable places. When these older theatres were built, PA sound systems didn't exist; therefore, all music was unamplified, so a space was designed where the band could be heard but not seen by the audience. The conductor had to be visible to the orchestra and the cast on stage. In addition, the sound of the orchestra had to be subdued a little as to not drown out the vocals on the stage. A pit was created at the front of the stage, which stretched underneath the stage with a space for the conductor on a riser at the front, where they could conduct the orchestra and the singers. This also allowed for the loudest instruments to be placed farther underneath the stage to better balance the sound in the auditorium. In the more modern theatres, the pits are often very sophisticated and have lifts and baffles for different scenarios. The pits can also be closed off totally and more seats sold at the front of the stage, literally on top of the pit. The majority of shows use the pit for the band, but on some productions the band can be either on stage or remoted. I will explain each of these in this chapter.

As mentioned, pits can often be very small. To fit in a large number of musicians, it can become very cramped, and the musicians are set up in a way that is totally different to how a band would set up on stage for a typical concert. I suppose the closest comparison would be working in a studio environment, where all the members of the band are separated to minimise spillage into each other's microphones.

THE PIT SETUP

A Live Pit Setup

The way a pit is set up will vary depending on the theatre, since every pit is different in size and shape. Usually the rhythm section, drums, bass, and guitars are grouped together on one side of the pit, and keyboards on the other, with any front-line brass, etc., wherever they fit. This is not always the case, though, since some pits are too small for the drummer and/or the percussion, so often they will have to be remoted elsewhere in the building (see the remote setup section). If possible, the musicians will be set up so that they can all see each other, and more importantly see the MD. Depending on the pit, this is not always possible, so visual monitors are used, and this is now becoming standard in the pit (see the monitoring section).

I will now talk you through the most common ways that a pit is set up for different instruments and what you can expect when having to play in the pit environment. There are of course many variants. depending on the theatre, the size of the band, the shape and size of the pit, etc., but this should give you some idea.

The MD

The MD is usually in the middle of the pit, raised up facing the stage, with his back to the audience. He or she is raised up enough so that they don't block the view of the audience of the stage, but high enough that they can see the stage clearly and the cast on stage can see them. In addition, it is common to have screens set up in the auditorium (usually on the front of the circle banister), showing the MD so that the cast can see the MD without having to be constantly looking directly at them. The cast may also have screens at the side of the stage with the MD visible. In theatres where there is no pit, the MD could be remoted with the rest of the band, and then the screens are the only way for the cast to see the MD. On a few occasions there is a small hole at the front of the stage where the MD will pop up through the stage and conduct from there, although this is rare.

Keyboards

Most shows these days use electronic keyboards rather than acoustic instruments, so acoustically they make very little noise. This means that the placement of the keys is not as big a concern as the drums, for instance, which are of course very loud acoustically. Modern shows often have more than one keyboard, which are grouped together in the pit if possible. If room allows, they will normally be placed facing the MD.

Guitars: Electric, Acoustic

The guitar setup varies greatly depending on the type of show. The sound designer or musical supervisor will often stipulate whether an amplifier is used, but the guitarist normally makes the decision on what effects and type of guitars they will use that are appropriate for the show.

Note

On the occasional show the guitarist will have to play specific equipment, guitars, and effects. This is usually because of a particular sound that the show needs or a specific look, if the guitarist is visible to the audience.

In a live pit, the guitarist will usually have an amplifier of some sort in the pit. Sometimes a split system is used where the amplifier is placed away from the pit. It is still mic'd up to create the same authentic guitar sound, but with less noise in the pit. The guitarist will have all his effects in the pit and will monitor the sound through the pit monitoring system using headphones or in-ears.

In a silent pit setup, the amplifier will be removed altogether and a direct feed will be taken from the guitar effects to the mixing desk, and then fed back through the pit monitoring system. However, digital effect processing for guitars is getting more and more sophisticated, and the use of amplifier simulators has meant that more and more guitarists are losing their amplifiers and going DI (direct input). See the Equipment chapter for more information.

Acoustic guitars are usually DI'd and do not use amplifiers. On occasion they might be mic'd up rather than using the built-in pickup, but that is usually the decision of the sound designer or sound operator on the show.

Bass Guitar

The bass guitar is in most cases DI'd, although a bass amplifier is sometimes used. There will sometimes be the need for some effect pedals and a volume pedal, but that is usually it. A double bass will need to be mic'd up, so a good-quality pickup on the bass will be needed. These will either be provided by the sound department or by the player.

Drums and Percussion

The drums and percussion department normally give the sound designer the most issues, since they are very loud instruments. The problem is that the sound from the instrument spills into the auditorium, which can make controlling the overall sound difficult. A booth is usually built around the drums and percussion to minimise the spillage as much as possible. If the drums and percussion are set up in the pit, they are normally in two separate booths, which on touring shows is usually built with transparent and soft soundproofing panels. On the stationary shows, like in the West End and on Broadway, a dedicated soundproof room is often built. These vary in quality, depending on the show, but

Working in a Pit Environment

will usually have their own air-conditioning and a window to see the MD or other members of the band.

Front Line: Saxophones, Trumpet, Trombones, etc.

These instruments can be another source of problems for the sound designer, since they can be very loud acoustically. They will also often be screened off, like the drums and percussion, to minimise spillage into the auditorium. If there is a front-line section, they will sit together if space allows, but may still be screened off from one other. When players are doubling or trebling on different instruments, it is common to have different microphones for each instrument. These will be turned off and on either by a foot switch that the player controls or by the sound operator.

Remote Setup

A remote setup is used for numerous reasons and can either be for the whole band or individual band members. It can be used when the pit is too small to accommodate the band, when there is no pit in the theatre, or when the producers have decided to close off the pit and sell more seats at the front of the stage, where the pit would normally be.

When individual band members are remoted, or the entire band, you will set up in another room in the theatre, often under the stage, but the normal pit setup will still be used. You will still monitor from the normal pit monitoring system and even be screened off in exactly the same way as you do in the pit, even the booth for the drums. The experience is very much the same as being in the pit, but you don't need to wear your pit attire, since you can't be seen by the audience. You may think that this doesn't make any sense. Why screen everything off when there is no spillage into the auditorium? The reason is that the sound department wants it to sound as close as possible to how it normally does in the pit, and they still want to eliminate spillage into microphones from different instruments. Just think of it as moving the pit into another room. On stationary shows, the same applies. All instruments are screened off from one other, with drums in a separate booth. The most similar scenario is working in a recording studio environment.

The biggest difference in being remoted is that you often can't hear any sound from the front-of-house PA or from the stage, and you sometimes can't even see the MD. This means you are totally reliant on your monitoring system for sound and for seeing the MD. So double-check that these are all working before you do a show in a remote environment. Being remoted can be a strange experience, and you can feel totally removed from the show environment, but if you treat it in the same way as being in the pit, you quickly adjust, and it shouldn't affect your playing much.

Silent Pit Setup

We've discussed a live pit setup, so what is a silent pit setup? The basic idea is that no sound can be heard from the pit in the auditorium. This doesn't just relate to bands in the pit, but also if the band is on stage, or wherever. The concept is that very little acoustic sound comes from the band, but how can this be achieved and why? The reason is that the sound designer is trying to have more control over the overall sound in the auditorium. The less acoustic sound that comes from the band, the more control of the band balance there will be. For instance, if there is a quiet scene in the show, and the sound operator turns down an acoustic band, there will be a point where the acoustic instruments, like drums and brass, etc., will be acoustically too loud for him to turn the rest of the band down any further. With a silent pit, this is not a problem, and in theory the sound operator can turn the band down to a whisper if needed. You may have noticed that I said 'in theory'; there is a reason for this, which I will go into in a bit.

So how can you make a pit silent? You use only electronic instruments, and you DI everything, so no amplifiers. The drums need to be electronic, for example Roland V-Drums. Guitars need to be DI'd directly from the effects module. As you can probably tell, there is a flaw in this plan. This can only work for bands that have certain instruments, and no instrument is totally silent. When I have done shows with this setup, there has never been any front line or percussion, since they cannot really be electrified. The other problem is the fact that electronic instruments like V-Drums still make a noise, which can be surprisingly loud. As soon as you throw acoustic guitars into the mix, it starts to become a pointless exercise. Having a silent pit is possibly a way to make the sound operator's life a little easier, although I think this is debatable, but I think it makes the musician's life much harder. As a drummer I never find playing in a silent pit as rewarding as when there are live instruments and an acoustic drum kit. Electronic instruments and effects are getting better all the time, and so is monitoring equipment, so that experience will possibly improve. When there is no pit or a very shallow pit in a venue, a silent pit setup is sometimes used for some of the band, but acoustic instruments like front line are still used alongside. This can often work well as a compromise.

If you do need to play in a silent pit environment, make sure that you have good monitoring and are comfortable with the instrument you have to use, in case it is provided for you. For example, if you are a drummer, a V-Drum kit could be provided. If you have never used one, try to borrow one to practise on so that you get used to the feel and sounds. Also, learn how to do basic programming. The same goes for guitarists using effects modules they are not familiar with.

Onstage Setup

Being on stage on a musical theatre show can take many forms. You could be set up like a traditional band on the stage facing the audience; you could be on a riser at the back of the stage; or you could be split up from the rest of the band in the wings or even within the set for the show. Many well known shows have the band as part of the action on stage, at least for some parts of the production. Shows like *Grease*, *Dirty Dancing*, *We Will Rock You*, and *The Rocky Horror Picture Show* have had the band set up at the back of the stage on a large riser above the performers. The band will often be hidden from view for parts of the show and then revealed for certain songs or scenes. Normal pit monitoring will most often be used, and acoustic screening is usually used, at least for drums and percussion. Although you are on stage, you will not be a big part of the action on the stage, and the

Working in a Pit Environment

experience is not that much different to being in the pit, although you may need to wear some sort of a costume and interact a little in some scenes.

Another scenario is when you are on the stage and are more part of the show. The *Jersey Boys* show is a good example of this, where you will — depending on your instrument — actually interact with the actors and will have some set choreography and costume changes. Don't worry, you will be rehearsed for any choreography and any lines or interaction you may have to do on stage, even if you are a dep.

The band could also be set up on movable scenery that can be moved onto the stage at certain parts of the show. If you are part of any movable scenery, just make sure that your equipment is properly secured, since stage scenery can often jolt unexpectedly when moved.

You could also be set up somewhere at the back of the stage or in the wings (the space on either side of the stage, out of view of the audience) and be out of sight for the entire show. This is sometimes done when there is no pit in the theatre. The band is then screened off, just as if they were in the pit, and often no amplifiers for guitar and bass will be used to try to keep the onstage volume down.

Whatever scenario is used, it is important to keep a few points in mind. If you are on stage and visible to the audience, it is very important to watch what you do when you are not playing. You need to look professional at all times, since the audience will most likely be able to see you the entire time. Make sure that you look presentable, whether you are dressed in black or any costume that you might need to wear. Make sure you don't make any noise when you're not playing, and this applies to when you are onstage or off, since any noise could potentially put off the performers and could be heard by the audience. Being onstage can often be more interesting than being in the pit, since you do feel more part of the show, and the fact that the audience can see you play can feel more rewarding than being boxed off under the stage. Just remember that you are now part of the look of the show, so make sure you embrace that and try to be as professional as you can.

COMMON PIT EQUIPMENT

Much of the equipment used in the pit environment has become standard across the industry, and you are likely to come across some of it frequently, although there will of course be some variations. It's probably not necessary to know every piece of equipment, but it can be useful to know the purpose and terms used for some of the more common equipment you will find in a theatre pit. To give you a general idea, I've put together a list of the most common equipment and its purpose.

Screening

All pits will have some sort of screening. Both solid screens and see-through acrylic screens will be used, as well as full purpose-built rooms that often house the drums and percussion. The most common make used, at least in the UK, for portable screening is ClearSonic Screens, which are often put together to form anything from a simple partition between players to full drum and percussion booths.

Working in a Pit Environment

Microphones

There are hundreds of different microphones available on the market today. They basically fall into three categories: condenser, dynamic, and ribbon. Ribbon you don't often see in theatre, since they can be very fragile and expensive. Condenser and dynamic are the most common. Without getting too technical, I will just explain the basic differences between the two and how they are used.

Condenser Microphone

Often used for drum overheads and wind instruments. They provide a more accurate and usually a better sound quality for the more complex sound sources. They come in large- and small-diaphragm variations. Small condenser microphones can be recognised by their slim profile and are often referred to as pencil microphones. They need phantom power to work, a small current that gets sent from the mixing console. Common large-diaphragm brands include AKG 414, Neumann U87, and the Audio-Technica AT2035. Small-diaphragm include Shure SM81, AKG C1000, and Audio-Technica 4021, just to name a few.

Dynamic Microphones

Frequently used on snare drums, bass drums, and louder instruments. They are also a popular choice for hand-held vocal microphones. They don't need phantom power to work. The most common dynamic microphones you'll come across without a doubt are the Shure SM58 and SM57, although there are numerous others available.

Headphones

The most common headphones used in a pit, if you are not using your own in-ear headphones, are the Sennheiser HP25 or the Beyerdynamic 100 and 150. Sony and AKG headphones are sometimes used. The Sennheiser HP25 probably give the best isolation from external noise, but if you need even better isolation, there are headphones available such as the Extreme Isolation and the Vic Firth headphones, which are great for drummers, particularly.

In-Ear Monitoring

There are many brands of in-ear monitoring now available; the choice is ever increasing, and cost is going down. When it comes to in-ear monitoring, there are two types you can go for.

Generic In-Ear Headphones

The generic type has different-size foam or rubber inserts. These are cheaper to buy and can be bought off the shelf but will probably not give the same amount of noise isolation and fit as the custom types. There are literally hundreds of headphones in this category, but the most notable for sound quality and durability would be the Shure SE range.

Custom In-Ear Headphones

There are numerous companies that provide custom in-ear monitoring, and what makes these different from the generic type is that they are moulded specifically to your ears. They give you extra comfort and added noise isolation. Most custom in-ear manufacturers also use very high-quality drivers in their headphones, which should give you fantastic sound quality across all the frequency ranges, which in turn will give you a better experience when playing your instrument. They range from a single driver to eight drivers per ear. Each driver is essentially like a mini speaker, with each driver delivering a certain range of sound frequencies. More drivers doesn't necessarily mean better sound or quality, so check out reviews and recommendations before buying.

The most notable in-ear manufacturers at the time of writing are Ultimate Ears, ACS Custom, 64 Audio, and Westone, but there are many others. Do some research on what best suits your needs and budget.

The problem that can arise when using in-ear monitoring is that it can eliminate a lot of the ambient sound, and you can start to feel very isolated, since you can't hear the natural sound of your instrument. Many brass and woodwind players refuse to use in-ear monitoring for that reason, since they find it hard to keep their instrument in tune and to hear the fine nuances that the instrument can make. This is also relevant for drummers, bass players, and percussionists, where you lose most, if not all of the natural acoustic sound of your instrument and are totally reliant on the sound coming from the microphones into your monitor mix. Some in-ear monitoring suppliers also offer products that have an acoustic vent in the design of their product. This allows some acoustic sound to enter the ear, as well as the sound from the in-ear drivers. This can be an option, although most come at a price.

Pit Monitoring

There are a few variations in how monitoring is done in a pit situation, and this is also determined by whether it's a silent pit or a live pit situation, and also what instruments are being used. However, it has become standard over the last few years to use personal digital mixers for audio monitoring. The personal monitoring system allows each musician to monitor each instrument in the pit and alter volume and balance for each instrument. Generic controls usually include tone control (bass and treble) and master volume. You can also mute and solo individual tracks, and the user can save personal mixes. This is useful when a different balance of instruments is needed between different parts of the show. Each track should be labelled by the sound department, showing which instrument is on which channel.

You will most likely find Aviom digital mixers or possibly the Roland, Digidesign, or Yamaha equivalent. These vary slightly in operation and features, but the basic concept is the same. Occasionally you will have analogue monitoring like a Q8 or Q12, but that is rare these days. They can all be connected to headphones, in-ears, or speakers for the final output.

The Aviom

The most common monitoring equipment that I have personally used is the digital monitoring system by Aviom. It is essentially a sixteen-channel digital mixer with a headphone out. To store a mix, press and hold the two buttons on the far left labelled 'Save' and then press one of the sixteen channel buttons. The channel buttons will flash in sequence to

Working in a Pit Environment

indicate that a mix has been stored. To recall a mix, press the 'Recall' button (the light on the button will flash). You then press the relevant channel button where you stored the mix, and the mix will be recalled. When the Aviom system is turned off and on, the default mix will default to channel 1. Check www.aviom.com for photos and the latest variations of their products.

Monitoring on Speakers/Wedges

It's rare to monitor through speakers in a show pit environment. This would potentially lead to all the volume coming from the pit being much louder and therefore harder to control in the auditorium. Sometimes MDs will have small speakers for their monitoring. This is done so that the MD can hear vocals on stage acoustically; the speakers then are used for his instrument and any other instruments in the pit that can't be heard acoustically. The MD will not wear any headphones for monitoring in this case, unless there is a click being used. If the band is on stage for the show, speaker monitoring could be used, but this is rare, since the volume of the band would inevitably drown out the sound of the singers on stage, which would then in turn need to be amplified, and then the overall volume on stage becomes very loud. Since the singers don't usually have any in-ear monitoring, there will usually be speakers placed on stage to give the performers monitoring of the band and vocals.

Whatever monitoring you use, try to get your mix as balanced and musical as you can. The sound department often has the ability to do a separate monitor mix to what is going out front of house. This is often referred to as a pre-fader mix. If this is possible, you can have separate eq, balance, and individual mic levels (for example on a drum kit) and even have your own reverb settings. This can give your mix a more lively and realistic quality, rather than the sound of the box that you will most likely be playing in. It is worth spending some time on this in the first sound check, since it can make a huge difference to your playing experience. If time is tight in the sound check, which is often the case, have a word with the sound department about whether it would be possible to come in early one day and do it then. Usually the sound department is helpful if they can find the time.

Use of Visual Monitoring

It is common practice in a pit environment to use visual monitors so that the band members can easily see the MD. These monitors are usually LCD screens, which are mounted on the music stand and are normally in black and white. This is done because most often the band members do not have a clear view of sight of the MD; that is due to the way a pit needs to be set up because of space restrictions and screening.

> **Tip**
>
> I prefer to have the screen monitor mounted just above my music so that I can read the music while also keeping a close eye on the MD.

If there are no screens provided, make sure that you set up with eye contact with as many of your band members as possible while having a clear line of sight with your MD. It's best if you can read your music and see the MD at the same time, as much as possible. Even if you do have a screen, try to implement this anyway, since it can work as a failsafe in case the monitor malfunctions. The pit can be a very unmusical place, so try to make the experience the best you can.

Pit Etiquette

On some shows there can be long gaps between times when you are playing your instrument. So what can you do in these gaps? What is okay and what isn't? This depends on a number of factors, the main one being how visible you are to the audience. You have to use your judgement in deciding what is acceptable and what isn't, and of course follow and respect any rules and requests made by your MD.

If you're not visible at all to the audience, you are okay to most things, as long as you are always ready to play when your next entry comes. Bear in mind that if you have microphones around you, they might still be live even when you're not playing, so keep noise to a minimum. You will most likely not have to wear your normal pit attire; however, some MDs insist on all musicians wearing it if they are in the pit, even if they can't be seen by the audience.

If you are visible to the audience, reading books is sometimes accepted as long as it is done subtly. I would not advise things like newspapers because of the noise the paper can make. I personally think that if some of the audience can see you reading, you should not do it. I think it looks unprofessional to be occupied with other things during the show. If you can't be seen at all, fine, but otherwise not. Think — it is only about two to three hours of your time, and you need to stay focused, so try to be as professional as you can for that time.

Note

On Broadway, the Local 802 contract states that no reading material is allowed in the pit apart from your musical score. Check with your conductor for any clarification and exceptions.

Phones and tablets are occasionally accepted in the pit, as long as they are in flight mode and on silent. On silent only is sometimes not enough, since the cell signal can interfere with some of the electrical equipment. This has now become the platform that many of us use to read books and magazines, and they can often be made more discreet than an actual book or magazine. But again, only if you can't be seen by the audience. If you decide to take your phone or tablet into the pit to use for reading, lowering the brightness of the display can be a good idea, and do not forget to put it into flight mode. It can be an embarrassing situation if your phone starts ringing midshow because you forgot.

Try to look professional at all times — simple things like not slouching over your instrument or in your chair, not yawning without covering up your mouth, etc. Things like

Working in a Pit Environment

that can look terrible from the audience's perspective. People spend a lot of money going to see shows, so do your best to be professional in your job. Remember that sometimes the cast can see you from the stage, so be aware of what you have on display on your stand, and your behaviour. Just because the audience can't see you, it doesn't mean that no one can.

Drinking anything other than water in bottles is usually not allowed. You have to be very careful about spilling any liquids, since there is a lot of electrical equipment around. Eating of any kind is not usually permitted in the pit during the show. Smoking is of course never allowed. Talking has to be kept to a minimum, since there are often microphones close by, and the audience could be sitting close enough to the pit to hear you.

Making Noise After the Auditorium Is Open to the Public

On most shows it is acceptable for musicians to make some noise before the performance starts. Tuning up instruments is usually fine, and some light warmup exercises. It is usually not acceptable for the band to be playing together any sort of recognisable tune or song that is audible to the audience.

On some shows it is requested that no sound comes from the band after the audience is in. This could be because of a certain mood that the show wants to set, or could just be a request from the theatre or the MD. Whatever the situation is, you must respect it and do any warmups in the dressing room or somewhere away from the pit where the audience can't hear you.

Be aware of the noise you are making when you're not playing while the show is running, especially in quiet parts of the show. When you're wearing in-ear monitoring you can often forget about the noise you can make, since you can't hear it with your headphones or in-ears on. This goes for tuning your instrument or having a squeaky chair, as well as coughing and any other acoustic noise. Remember that the front row of the audience could be only a foot away, so if you have to make some noise like tuning your instrument, try to choose moments when you are the least likely to disturb the show or an audience member.

PIT ATTIRE

If you are at all visible to the audience from where you sit in the pit, you will need to wear the requested pit attire, which is usually all-black clothing. These are often referred to as 'blacks.' Some MDs/conductors are very specific about what sort of blacks you wear, while others are very relaxed about it. Sometimes the fixer/musical contractor will specify what you should wear. Whatever is specified you need to follow. A common specification is a black collared shirt, black trousers, and black smart shoes. Make sure that you have these in your arsenal, regardless. Short-sleeved shirts are usually allowed, and sometimes black t-shirts, especially if it's warm in the pit. If there is no specification to what sort of blacks you need to wear, at least make sure that you look reasonably smart, as emphasised earlier in the book. It's all just common sense — just make sure that you are always well presented.

Working in a Pit Environment

Note

The Broadway CBA contract states that musicians must wear jackets and ties during performances unless otherwise permitted by the employer/producer. Check for exact requirements from your conductor or contractor before the first performance.

There are occasions when you will need to wear some sort of a costume in the pit. This will usually go in line with the theme of the show and can include having to wear a tuxedo, a suit and tie, or a waistcoat. These sorts of costumes are more commonly used when the band is visible on stage but can also be used if the band is partially visible in the pit. Anything specific other than your basic blacks will usually be provided by the show. If you have to wear specific clothing that is provided, it will also be maintained and washed by the wardrobe department on the show. You just hand them in at the end of each show, or at an agreed interval, to be washed. The clothes will then be brought back to your dressing room ready for the next performance. Sometimes the wardrobe department will also wash your normal blacks, but don't assume that they will. On most occasions the wardrobe department is very busy and will not have time to be dealing with the musicians' clothes. At the start of a contract it can be worth asking the head of wardrobe if they would mind washing the musicians' clothes on occasion, say, once a week. A bottle of wine and some chocolates will go along way in showing your gratitude.

Setting Up and Packing Up

You are in most cases responsible for setting up and packing down your equipment, but this can depend on your instrument. If you are using your own equipment, it is your responsibility to get your instrument set up at the start of a venue and packed down into its cases at the end. The sound department and stage management will usually manage getting your equipment onto the transports to the next venue and will offload them at the other end, ready for you to set up again. If your instrument does not travel with the transports, it is of course your responsibility to get all your equipment in and out of the theatre. On a touring show this will happen every time the show moves to a new town or venue, but in the West End or on Broadway this only happens at the start and end of your contract.

If you are playing equipment that belongs to the production, sometimes the sound department will handle that for you, and you can just finish playing the show and head off. However, on occasion you are still required to get the instrument into its case, so double-check this at the start of the contract so you know the arrangement. Just make sure that you have done your duty and that all your equipment is properly packed up and is in an obvious place for the sound department to see.

6

Who's Who in Theatre

The theatre personnel structure can be quite complex, and as a musician you don't have to know the ins and outs of it, but it can be good to have a basic knowledge of who does what and who to speak to for certain things.

There are essentially three camps when it comes to theatre:

1. The people who are employed directly with the show full-time

2. The off-site staff who work for the producer and the creatives

3. The theatre staff who work directly for the theatre

The people who are employed directly with the show will be on the producers' payroll and will handle the everyday running of the show; they will move with the show if touring. The creative team are mainly involved in setting up the show but may pop in to check on things once in a while. The front-of-house staff like ushers and bar and ticket staff, as well as the local stage crew, which includes the fly men and master carpenter, are usually employed by the theatre itself. On a touring show this staff will be different in each venue as the show moves from one theatre to the next.

Normally the highest-ranking people in musical theatre are the money people, the producers. They will hire a creative team to get the show into production.

The Creative Team

Producer: The people with the money, responsible for financing anything to do with the show.

Director: In charge of the overall look of the show and creating a piece of theatre that tells the story in a convincing way.

Musical Supervisor: In charge of all things musical in the show.

Choreographer: Creates and teaches all the dance moves and any other physical movement on stage.

Sound Designer: Designs and specs all the sound equipment needed for the show. This included the front-of-house PA system, the pit setup, onstage monitoring, and also makes sure that the system fits in and works for every theatre being performed in, if the show is touring.

Production Manager: Is in charge of getting the show up and running in every theatre it needs to perform in. This includes getting all the set to fit in each theatre and making sure everything works when it comes to any flying set pieces or automation needed for the show. They have overall supervision over everything that involves the production and are usually in charge of hiring the technical team.

PERSONNEL WORKING DIRECTLY WITH THE SHOW

The creative team will then hire people to work on a daily basis to keep the show that they have created consistent. The structure in the UK is as follows:

Show Management Team

Every show will have a team of people who work behind the scenes and are in charge of the everyday running of the show. From the business side of things to the many things needed to make the show happen, both during a performance and either side of it, on and off stage, this team is crucial to any show's success.

Company Manager

The company manager is in charge of the entire company and is the communicator between artistic staff, actors, producers, and technicians. They handle the business side of the production, including the payroll for the cast and crew. On touring shows they will organise some of the logistics of getting the company from one theatre to the next and will communicate with each theatre on the touring schedule.

Stage Manager

The stage manager is in charge of everything that happens on the stage and has a team of assistants that coordinate the artistic side of the show. As well as overseeing everything on the stage, the stage manager will also have their own 'track' (duties) during the performance alongside the deputy stage manager and assistant stage managers. Other duties of the stage manager are to manage the get-ins and outs and the assembly of the show's set. The stage management team also manages any rehearsals scheduled.

DSM Deputy Stage Manager

The DSM is second in charge on the stage and will most likely cover the stage manager when they are not there. The DSM will 'call the show.' They normally sit in the wings (side of the stage, out of sight from audience) in front of the prompt desk, a control desk with screens, where they can see the stage with cameras in the auditorium, including an infrared camera for blackouts, and they call in the scenery and lights on and off at the correct times. They have a headset they use to communicate with the stage crew, stage manager, ASMs, fly men, and light and sound crew, and they instruct them when to bring scenery in and out and when lights need to come on and off, etc. Basically, they control the flow of the show as the audience sees it. During rehearsals, the DSM will create the prompt book, which becomes the blueprint to how the show will run, when scenery moves and lighting cues happen, as well as members of the cast entering the stage. DSMs usually have their own personal way of creating the book, and this can be done either directly to orchestral arrangement of the show, or they will have some sort of a shorthand way of notating the cues, but they will in most cases be related to the music in the show. The DSM is also responsible for any backstage announcements, which include the thirty-minute, fifteen-minute, five-minute, and beginners calls to notify cast, crew, and musicians when the show is ready to start.

ASM Assistant Stage Manager

ASMs take instruction from the DSM and stage manager and are normally in control of all props for the show, as well as moving scenery about and instructing cast members to be ready for their entries. There are normally at least two ASMs on a show, one on each side of the stage, and they oversee that part of the stage.

Broadway and US Variations

The roles of stage management are a little different on Broadway, and people's titles have slight variations. The person in charge on a Broadway show is the production stage manager, or the head stage manager. They are in charge of organising the stage management team and are in charge of calling the show, or 'running the book,' as it's sometimes referred to on Broadway, as well as backstage announcements and organising rehearsals. The second in command is the stage manager, and next in line would be the assistant stage manager, who has the same responsibilities as the ASM in the UK. The production stage manager is often just referred to as the stage manager, and the next in line is the first assistant stage manager and then the second assistant stage manager. A Broadway musical requires at least three people on the stage management team, and a play at least two.

ON-SITE CREATIVE TEAM

The creative team will most often employ resident creatives to oversee the show for them on a daily basis. It is common for these to be part of the actual company and be in the show, either as covers (swings) or as part of the cast. On Broadway the production stage manager will sometimes also double as the associate director, if they are qualified to do so.

Resident Director

If a show has appointed a resident director, they will be in charge of maintaining the work of the director consistently throughout every performance. They will give notes to the cast relating to any performance-related issues and will run any rehearsals needed for training up understudies for their cover roles.

Dance Captain

A dance captain is there to make sure that any dancing and movement on stage is kept consistent and at the same high level as the choreographer intended. They will also run rehearsals with the director to train the understudies and any cleanup calls needed to keep the show up to standard.

TECHNICAL TEAM

Sound Team

The sound team will have the sound operator operating the sound desk front of house. The other team members will most likely be onstage or backstage helping out and managing microphones, etc. The number of people in the sound team can vary depending on the size and complexity of the show, but two or three is common.

Sound Number 1: In charge of the sound team and normally operates the sound desk.

Sound Number 2: Is sound number one's cover and will handle sound matters on stage during the performance.

Sound Number 3: A general sound assistant. May deal with microphones for the cast and other general sound issues.

LX Team In charge of all light and effects on the show. Can be a team of one to three, depending on the show. Sometimes extra specialists will be brought in if the show has special effects, including pyro effects (explosives) and if there is flying — where members of the cast get flown around the stage in harnesses.

THE MUSIC TEAM

The music team includes the musical supervisor and fixer/contractor, but they will not usually be directly involved with the running of the show, unless the musical supervisor and the MD is one and the same, or the MD is also the fixer. The team will commonly consist of the following:

- **Musical Supervisor** (See Chapter 2)
- **Fixer or Musical Contractor** (See Chapter 2)
- **Musical Director** (See Chapter 7)
- **Assistant Musical Director** (See Chapter 7)
- **The Band**

IN-HOUSE PERSONNEL

The in-house personnel work for the theatre directly and will therefore be different in each venue on a touring show.

Local Stage Crew and Fly Team

The fly team is responsible for operating the flying equipment in the theatre. That means they bring in and out any curtains or set pieces that are flown in from above the stage. They will take cues from the DSM (the production stage manager in the US) when each piece is flown in or out. Modern theatres will often use electronically operated flies, but older theatres will still use manually operated ropes and pulleys. Other local stage crew personnel will also work with the show's stage management team to assist with moving scenery and any other stage-related tasks.

Master Carpenter

The carpenter is responsible for any maintenance work onstage that involves carpentry. Bigger production may have their own carpenter to deal with any set maintenance.

Front-of-House Staff

Box office, ushers, and bar staff are responsible for the running of the box office, bars, and for getting the audience seated for the performance.

ONSTAGE TEAM

These are the people who will be on stage during a performance:

- Stage Management Team
- Resident Creative Team
- Cast

- Swings
- Fly men
- Local stage crew

7

The Musical Director (MD)/Conductor

Many musicians start playing in a band situation, where there is usually no real bandleader and very rarely an actual conductor. They follow the drummer for the time, and the drummer is often the one counting you into the song. If you have worked with a Big Band or in a more classical setting, you will most likely have experience of working with a conductor. However, if have never worked with an MD, it can be a very different experience to what you are used to.

THE MUSICAL DIRECTOR/CONDUCTOR

In a musical, the musical director (MD), or the conductor, is the person in charge of anything music-related in the show. They answer to the musical supervisor, but the musical supervisor does not normally deal with the day-to-day running of the show. They will normally depart after the production period and leave the show in the hands of the MD. The MD is part of the creative team and will work closely with the resident director, the dance captain, and the stage management team to make sure that the show runs smoothly on a daily basis.

The role of the MD is complex and covers not just band-related things but also what is happening onstage, as well as making sure that all vocals are correct. They are also responsible for a vocal warmup before every show for the cast. This is normally done on stage about sixty to ninety minutes before the show. If there are two shows that day, the vocal warmup only happens before the first show. An MD has also many duties and things to deal with that may not be directly music-related. When working with a big cast of singers, dancers, and musicians there can often be clashes of personalities, and personal politics start to creep in, especially on the long-running shows. Therefore, an MD also has to be a good people person and mediator.

THE ASSISTANT MD/ASSOCIATE CONDUCTOR

The MD usually has an assistant who helps out with things like vocal warmups and will step up to conduct the show when the MD wants to do a show watch or have some time off. A dep will then be booked for the assistant MD's chair to cover their part, and this will be paid by the company. A show watch is a chance for the MD to see the show from the audience's perspective and to hear the band from the auditorium through the PA system. The MD can then give notes to the cast and band on things that can be changed or improved for the benefit of the show. Show watches are normally scheduled in every few weeks, or the MD can request one if they feel it's needed. On most shows the assistant will conduct shows on a regular basis so that they are always prepared for any emergencies if the MD can't do a show.

The Types of MD

Depending on the show, the MD's role can be different. Some shows require an MD that plays an instrument, while some will require an MD that purely conducts in a more classical way. I will explain a little about each and what you need to be aware of as a musician.

The Playing MD

An MD that plays an instrument is the most common in modern musicals. The main reason is that it allows the band to be smaller when the conductor can play one of the parts. The most common instrument for an MD tends to be the keyboard but can on occasion be the guitar, or even drums on rare occasions.

The disadvantage of a playing MD is that they will have their hands tied to playing their instrument and therefore can't always conduct that easily. Many MD's revert to conducting by nodding their head while playing or playing with one hand while conducting with the other. This can take some co-ordination, so if you're striving to be an MD, make sure you practise this skill.

Stick MD — Conducting Only

When an MD does not play an instrument, they are often referred to as 'Stick MD.' This derives from the conductor's baton they use to conduct, which is often referred to as 'the stick.' The stick MD comes from the classical tradition of an

The Musical Director / Conductor

orchestral conductor and is more commonly used in the more traditional musical theatre shows, although not exclusively. Here the MD's role is conducting only, and they will usually conduct through all of the music, so the band and cast can follow their every move. When there is a rhythm section playing, this can on occasion become more for show than for timekeeping purposes, but the MD can still decide to move the tempo if they so wish.

FOLLOWING AN MD

As a musician working with an MD, you have to learn each MD's way of conducting and interpret their gestures correctly. The conducting from a playing MD can sometimes be less obvious than a stick conductor, so try to understand and learn how they communicate their conducting.

> **Tip**
>
> If you're having difficulty in accurately placing a cue from an MD, try to figure out from what they are getting their cue. It could be a vocal cue, for instance, so try to listen for that cue, and then you can possibly anticipate what the MD is doing.

Things to Be Aware of When Working With an MD

1) Learn where the conductor's downbeat is. MDs can conduct in very different ways, and their downbeat can be portrayed in different places. For

instance, more classically trained conductors may place their downbeat on their actual upbeat, which is usually to allow the strings in an orchestra to strike the bow before the note actually sounds. This can be rather off-putting and odd in a more modern band setup, so try to understand where they want the note to sound in relation to their conducting.

1) The MD is in charge. You need to be sensitive to what the MD is doing, and you need to make sure that you watch them closely at all times. Unexpected things can happen that you can't see from where you are in the pit, and the MD might need to correct or slightly move the tempo to compensate for what is happening onstage. Even if the MD does something that seems unmusical or is not written in the part, they will (usually) have a good reason for doing so; you need to follow and not question their authority. Remember that the MD has a lot to think about, so be as supportive and alert as you can be. Just bear in mind that a conductor is often more concerned with what's happening onstage than in the pit, so if they start waving their arms frantically, which doesn't bear any resemblance to the music, they probably haven't lost the plot but are trying to help out a singer on stage who's lost their way. You just need to know when you need to follow and what is relevant to you; this you will learn with experience.

2) Respect and diplomacy. The MD is the boss, whether you like it or not, so be professional and show them respect and do your job to the best of your ability at all times, even if you don't like them all that much. You

are there as a professional, so address issues in a respectable and sensitive way. It will reflect better on you to be diplomatic than to be a rebel and cause friction in the band.

BEING AN MD/CONDUCTOR

Being an MD on a show can be a tough job, and you need to have numerous skills to be successful. Whether you are an MD that plays an instrument while conducting, or you just conduct, playing and conducting will probably be the least of your worries when working in musical theatre. You are responsible for anything that is musical in the show, and you need to make sure that everything is consistently correct, in tune, and in time, both onstage and off. This goes for the cast onstage, the band in the pit, and also anything else music-related, like a backing track or anything that has an impact on the overall sound of the show.

As an MD/Conductor, you have many other duties that are not necessarily music-related, and you will have to deal with people from all different departments that are involved in the show running smoothly.

The Skills Needed as an MD/Conductor on Shows

The skills you need are varied and numerous, but here are some of the ones I believe are crucial to master and to be aware of if you are going to have a successful career as a musical director.

- Have a good understanding of vocal control and singing technique.

- Have good co-ordination and be able to conduct in time while playing.
- Have good control of conducting with a baton in a clear manner.
- Have good people skills. Be diplomatic and a good mediator.
- Have a good understanding of the theatre machine and its personnel.
- Have good knowledge of different musical styles.
- Have some musical arrangement skills.
- Have some knowledge of electronic instruments, keyboards, and sound modules.
- Have some knowledge of popular software used in theatre, like QLab and MainStage, just to name a couple.

Tip

Practice conducting in front of a mirror to determine whether you are giving a clear enough beat to follow. Practise conducting with both hands so that you can play with either hand at the same time. Find a comfortable way to give some sort of time while playing with both hands, using head gestures.

The Musical Director / Conductor

Earn Your Respect

If you want to have a good relationship with your fellow musicians, cast, and creative team, treat everyone with respect. When you need to give notes or instructions, try to do it in a sensitive way. Try to give people notes privately, and if it's a group note, make sure it doesn't get directed at any individual or could be taken as such. People can be sensitive and paranoid, and unconstructive criticism can be counterproductive and make that person nervous and self-conscious, which can in turn make their performance worse.

Speak up and stand your ground on matters that you feel strongly about, but try not to lose your temper. It reflects badly on you and will be counterproductive in achieving the results you want. Always be calm and professional. Get people to respect you for being good at what you do and be supportive. If you feel out of your depth, seek advice and improve on things in your own time.

The Rehearsal Process

As an MD, your job is also to rehearse with all the cast and teach them all their vocal lines. The rehearsals will often start many weeks before the first performance and can be on an extremely hectic schedule. Prior to that, you might also be involved in the audition process, when the cast are being selected for the relevant parts in the show. Along with the musical supervisor, you need to make sure that everyone who is cast is suitable for the job and can sing in the range for which their part is written, and do it to a high enough standard, eight times a week.

When rehearsals start, it's your job, with the help of your assistant, to get the cast ready and memorising all their vocal lines. The more experienced singers will do this quickly, while others might struggle. Get everyone to record their individual harmony lines using a Dictaphone (usually a smartphone these days) and then go away and learn to memory. There will be a strict schedule in rehearsals, which the DSM/stage manager will be in charge of, and time will be split up between the different departments, including music, choreography, and the director. Everyone wants as much time as possible for their parts, so make sure you request and fight for the time necessary for you to get everything done in time.

The show is normally rehearsed in stages and sometimes not even in the correct order. It will then be stitched together, and then a run of both acts will be done with stops and starts. The last few days of the rehearsals will normally just include runs of the show, with the occasional sectional rehearsal thrown in. Some of the show props will be in the rehearsal room to help, and even pieces of the actual set. During the rehearsal process many changes can happen to the show and the music, so as an MD you will need to be adaptable and be able to implement changes quickly. However, if you feel that something does not work musically, do voice your opinion and try to come to a better solution. When the rehearsal period is finished, which can last many weeks or even months, it will be time to move to the theatre for technical rehearsals. I cover this in more detail in the next chapter.

8

A Week in the Life of a Show Musician

To give you an idea of what the lifestyle of a professional musician in theatre is like, I thought I would give you an example of how a typical week might play out. This does vary, depending on whether the show is stationary, like in the West End or Broadway, or if it's touring, and if the show is in its early stages of being set up. The setup stage, or the production period, is a much busier time with rehearsals and technical rehearsals, but when the show is up and running, most weeks are similar in how they run. I will give you an example of a week on a West End show and a touring show. I will then give you a quick rundown of a production period and how that could play out.

These examples are based on my personal experiences and can vary for different shows and depending on where you are based. We are all individuals and have different lives, commitments, and priorities, so how you would plan your week might be totally different; however, this will give you some idea of how the routine of the shows can work.

A Week in the Life of a West End Musician

Working in the West End of London or on Broadway is probably the dream of most show musicians. It is about as high you can go as a musician in the industry. You are working in a vibrant and exciting city where you can socialise with many fellow musicians, plus you can commute from home, assuming you live in or around the city. Many musicians I know have different reasons for wanting to be in the big cities like London. Some have had the ambition of working in the West End since they started to play their instrument, some want it for the money, and some just want to be at home and not to be touring. Whatever the reason, working in the West End is always fun and very different to touring. I must mention that for MDs or an assistant MD, this will be slightly different, since they have added duties that the other musicians don't. They will normally need to be in the theatre much earlier than the rest of the musicians to do extra rehearsals and the vocal warmup for the cast.

The show is now up and running, and all technical rehearsals and sound checks are done. The show runs with eight shows every week. As we talked about earlier, the typical show times are an evening show Monday to Saturday, and then two matinees, one always on a Saturday and the other midweek.

I always make sure to get into the town centre at least an hour before the show starts, allowing for any delays with trains or traffic, depending on the mode of transport. When

A Week in the Life of a Show Musician

in the theatre the routine is similar from day to day. The cast and crew will have been in the theatre much earlier to get everything ready for the show, and the MD, or assistant MD, will conduct a vocal warmup on stage about an hour before the show.

For a 7:30 p.m. show, the thirty-minute call is made at 6:55 p.m. by the deputy stage manager. All the cast have to be in the building now, have signed in, and are not allowed to leave the building. I head to the band dressing room, and I get changed into my blacks. The fifteen-minute call is made. I then go to the pit and check that everything is okay with my equipment and my monitoring. Some of the band members are already warming up their instruments. The five-minute call is made, then beginners is called. The rest of the band is now in the pit, as well as the MD. The MD gives a standby, and the whole band goes silent. There is a front of house announcement made about how no recording equipment can be used. The MD counts the band in.

NOTE

All the preshow calls made are five minutes early in relation to the show start time. So if the show is due to start at 7:30, the thirty-minute call is at 6:55; the fifteen-minute call is at 7:10; the five is at 7:20, and beginners is at 7:25.

We finish the first half of the show and are now in the interval (or intermission in North America). The interval is typically twenty minutes long. The DSM will call a five-minute call and then beginners to act 2.

The show finishes about 10:00 p.m., and I head back to the band room to get changed out of my blacks. I will either head straight home or on occasion go for a quick drink with the band/cast.

In the West End and on Broadway, the show schedule will be pretty much the same each day. Of course, on a matinee day you will need to get there earlier in time for the afternoon show. In between shows you will normally go out for some food with your band mates or whatever you choose for the couple of hours you have to kill. The majority of shows have a six-day working week, so you will have a scheduled day off each week. This will land on a Sunday in many cases, unless your show has scheduled Sunday shows, in which case your day off could land on another day of the week.

You can see that a typical week in the West End of London is usually straightforward. You have most of your days free, and musicians use this time in different ways. Many will teach, either in local schools or from home, do other session work, and spend time with family and friends. It's also common for musicians to take a show off every now and again, sometimes even one or two a week, to do other gigs or projects. This is helpful to keep you enthusiastic about your regular show and to stop you going stagnant in your playing, since playing the same show eight times a week can take its toll. There will be the occasional rehearsals called in the week, but usually the band will not be required. The MD and assistant MD will run these, which are most commonly to rehearse understudies for the cast.

A Week in the Life of a UK Touring Musician

The life of a touring musician can be very different from a West End or a Broadway musician, or indeed anywhere where you are working for a long period of time in the same venue that is commutable to your home.

When touring, there is much more going on and many things to organise. (I go into this in more detail in the 'Touring' chapter). You are often in a different city every week, and you need to get yourself there, organise digs, and support yourself with food away from your home comforts, and a kitchen in many cases. I'm going to give an example of a typical week on a weekly UK tour. I will have booked my digs many weeks in advance and have looked at the best way to get to the venue. In this example I am staying in a hotel, so without any cooking facilities, and I have decided to drive and not use public transport.

Monday — Get-in Day

I need to be at the theatre to set up no later than 3:00 p.m., and Google Maps tells me it will take me three hours to get there. I will give myself an extra hour just in case there are any traffic issues and for a quick coffee stop. In the morning I finish packing my bag for the week. I made sure on the Sunday that all my clothes were washed and ready. I have breakfast, and about 9:30, after the rush hour traffic has died down a little, I check the traffic on Google Maps. If there are any accidents reported or other traffic issues, I may need to leave earlier. The car is fuelled and ready to go. I load my bags and head off.

    Before leaving, I would also have checked where I can park the car. Some hotels don't have any parking facilities, so make sure you have a plan, otherwise it can get very costly. You can use Google Street View to locate residential streets with no parking restrictions. Some hotels have parking, but they can be expensive if staying for long periods. I arrive in the city having been delayed slightly by some traffic, I check in and then go straight to the theatre. I sign in at stage door and head down to the pit to set up. All the other band members are also setting up their instruments, and the sound department is busy helping. Onstage, the cast are having their vocal warmup, and departments are busy getting ready for this evening's show. The assistant MD hands out the pad to all the band members.

Note

The sound team, stage management, and most other departments would have been in the theatre since early that morning, or even the day before, to set up the stage, including lights and sound systems. When the musicians rock up just before sound check, don't be surprised if there are a few tired and cranky sound personnel about, so try to be a little understanding if they are not at your beck and call — they often work very long hours.

A Week in the Life of a Show Musician

At 4:00 p.m. the sound check starts. We start with the drums and then move on to every instrument in the pit individually. We then play a couple of numbers from the show as a band and adjust our monitoring to suit. The MD asks if everyone's happy with their sound. The cast then is asked to say a few lines individually to test their microphones, and we play a few numbers from the show with the cast. Normally, we play one song that features each of the principals (the leads) in the show, and then a couple that have everyone singing.

The sound check finishes at 6:00 p.m., and we head off to get some food before the show. Some of the other band members head off to check in to their digs. I head back to the theatre for 7:00 p.m. and get changed into my blacks. We get the fifteen-minute call. We have a quick chat in the band room, and then I warm up for a few minutes in the pit. We get the five-minute call and then beginners. The MD checks the click before we start to make sure that we all have it in our monitoring. The MD gives a standby. We start the show.

Note

The actual running of the show, like the vocal warmups, half an hour calls, etc., is pretty much the same whether you are working in the West End or on tour; it's more your life around it that is different. As soon as you are in the theatre, there really is no real difference in how things are run. On touring shows there will just sometimes be fewer facilities for band members and cast because of size of the theatre. Since the show is only there for a week or two, not much gets done about it, and people just put up with it for the short period. In the West End, money would usually be spent on fixing the issues, because the show would be expected to be there for many months or even years.

After the show I change back out of my blacks, and there is a free drink provided by the theatre in the front of house bar. Cast, crew, and band gather there for a quick drink. This is common practise in many theatres in the UK, where the theatre will organise a free drink for a new show after their first performance. People then head off to their digs or go on for more drinks or food.

Tuesday

I find a local store to buy a few essentials for my room and then head out to get some lunch. In the afternoon I go to the gym with which the theatre has a deal.

Note

Check the theatre notice board for any gym deals and discounts at local restaurants. Also, check the touring chapter about tips for saving money on tour.

A Week in the Life of a Show Musician

I have a little explore of the city and then go for dinner with some of the guys from the band before the show. The show routine is as normal.

Note

There will be things happening onstage on most days, equipment and set maintenance, rehearsals for the cast or vocal warmup. So be respectful if you are practising on your instrument that you are not disturbing anyone working on stage or in the auditorium. Check with stage management first whether it's okay for you to practise and make some noise.

Wednesday

Much the same as Tuesday, but there are two shows today, so I head straight to the theatre after lunch.

Show goes as normal.

We head for dinner between shows.

We do the show again.

Go to pub for a couple of drinks with the band and cast.

The Show Musician

Note

There can often be more social life on tour than in the West End, since everyone is away from home. In the West End the majority of people just head straight home after the show, although there are of course exceptions to this.

Thursday

A lazy day and a gym session. Get food before show.

The show routine is as normal.

Back to hotel.

Friday

There is a day out planned to check out a local attraction.

The show routine is as normal.

Head off to a local jazz bar for some live music.

Saturday

Pack my bag and check out of the hotel.

Do lunch and the matinee performance.

I have some food and then do the evening show. In the interval I get all my cases ready for the packdown after the show. The quicker you can pack down, the sooner you'll be on the road and back home in your bed. Most touring musicians have this perfected to save every second of packdown time.

A Week in the Life of a Show Musician

As soon as the show finishes, I start packing my equipment away. I get it done in twenty minutes. I go to my car and set off for home, checking the traffic and whether there are any road closures on my route. In the UK it is common for many roads to be closed for maintenance work on a Saturday night, so check before leaving to avoid long diversions and delays. Use Google Maps traffic and The Highway Agency website to check.

Note

Some members of the cast, crew, and band will decide not to travel home on their day off but to head straight to the next city. This will of course depend on your circumstance and lifestyle. Your travel allowance does not account for you travelling home between venues, so that will be at your own expense. In the bigger countries like the United States, it's in most cases not possible to travel home between cities, so it is standard just to stay on tour for the duration of the contract.

Sunday

I unpack my bag, get the washing done, and repack, ready for another week away. I spend the rest of the day with the family. On Monday the routine starts again.

Note

Some weeks you can commute from home, if the city the show is in that week is close enough. I normally commute anything that's within a ninety-minute drive. Sometimes you can also use public transport like trains; just make sure there is a train coming back late in the evening. For the farther venues, over a four-hour drive, I will normally fly if there is an airport nearby. This does, however, mean that you will need digs for an extra night, since there is not normally a flight back after the last show on the Saturday night, so you'll need to fly back Sunday morning. The same applies for trains, at least in the UK.

THE TECH WEEK/PRODUCTION PERIOD

The tech week is much busier than a normal show week and is structured very differently, so I thought I would give you a quick insight into how it all works. The tech week is when the show is out of the rehearsal stage and has moved into the theatre where it will open, and all the departments come together to make the show ready for its opening night. This is based on my personal experience and can vary from show to show, but here is a quick breakdown of how a tech week could possibly play out, leading into the first performance.

A Week in the Life of a Show Musician

Monday

Usually there will be a band call in the theatre on the first day. This is usually when the band meets for the first time. The call is normally about 10:00 a.m., so I will book some digs from the Sunday night so that I can get into the theatre early enough to set up. In the West End I would try to get my equipment there on the Sunday to avoid the Monday rush-hour traffic. I then just get the train in on the Monday morning. On tour I drive up the night before and stay over.

I arrive at the theatre about 9:00 a.m. and set up my equipment.

At ten we have a quick sound check. Often these band calls will have just normal PA equipment, so bring earplugs like you would for a normal live gig situation, just in case it gets loud.

The personnel at these band calls normally includes:

- The musical supervisor
- The fixer/musical contractor
- The keyboard programmer (See 'Equipment' chapter)
- The sound designer or one of his/her representatives
- The band

Sometimes the arranger or a copyist will be there to make adjustments to the music, especially if it's a new show

The Show Musician

or a show that has been rewritten or altered from previous versions. Occasionally the composer will be there also.

Note

As you can see, in the first band call there are some extremely influential people present, and this can be the first time they have met you, and, more importantly, heard you play. So make sure to prepare for the band call. Try your best to get the pad before the event and listen to any recording you can get your hands on. Often the sound in these calls is not great, and it can be difficult to hear the other members of the band. There will be no vocals to guide you. So make sure you know the music extremely well before the call. You don't want to be the one getting it wrong.

The band will then play through the pad with stops and starts to check that everything is okay in the pad and to determine if there are any issues. The calls are booked in three-hour sessions, so the first will be from 10:00–1:00 p.m., an hour for lunch and then call two from 2:00–5:00 p.m., two hours for dinner, and the third call from 7:00–10:00 p.m. There aren't always three sessions in the day, but it can happen.

Tuesday

10:00 a.m. Sitzprobe

A Week in the Life of a Show Musician

A Sitzprobe is when the cast will join the band and play through all the music in the show. This is often a really fun moment and the only time that the cast and creatives will hear the music played acoustically. As soon as the band is in the pit, the whole dynamic changes and the organic energy that a live band produces diminishes. This is also when you get to meet the cast for the first time, if you have not been involved in the rehearsal process, and is the only time that the cast get to see the band play (unless you are onstage for the show), and you get to see the cast sing. This can give everyone involved a real sense of each other's roles in the show.

After the Sitzprobe, the band will need to move their equipment into the pit or stage.

The next call will then be for a band sound check in the pit or stage. This is often a full three-hour call.

Wednesday

10:00 a.m.–1:00 p.m. Tech rehearsal, MD and drums only

It is common to have the MD and drums present for the tech rehearsals to give the cast and choreographer a more definite rhythm and tempo so that they can block (the way the performers are organised on the stage and use the space so that it looks good and symmetrical) the show more accurately. The rest of the band is not called for the tech rehearsals, so they can go home. This is usually to save the producers money, which is understandable since the production period is a highly expensive period for the producers, possibly before any tickets have been sold.

    2:00–5:00 p.m. Tech rehearsal

    7:00–10:00 p.m. Tech rehearsal

Thursday

    10:00 a.m.–1:00 p.m. Tech rehearsal

    2:00–5:00 p.m. Tech rehearsal

    7:00–10:00 p.m. Dress rehearsal — full band called

Friday

    2:00–5:00 p.m. Dress rehearsal

    7:30–10:30 p.m. First performance

Saturday

    14:30 Matinee performance

    19:30 Evening performance

The first few performances are often referred to as preview performances, and tickets are sometimes sold at a discount. This is time allocated to let the show settle and to iron out any potential issues before the press night, when the all the press is invited to see the show and the important press reviews are done. In the West End and on Broadway, these preview performances can often go on for a few weeks, or even months, before the official opening performance and press performance.

A Week in the Life of a Show Musician

There will normally be at least another two to four performances before a press performance, even on a touring show. So in this example the press night would most likely be on the Tuesday night. It is usual for a party to be thrown by the producer after the show on the press night, which all the cast, crew, and band, as well the press, producers, and creatives can attend. Depending on the show, these events can be anything from a free drink in the front-of-house theatre bar to a massive event in a hired venue, with live music and celebrities roaming the floors.

So I hope this gives you some general idea of what a week in the life of a show musician is like. As you can see, there is not much to it. As soon as the show is up and running, it becomes a normal routine, like most jobs. I can of course only speak from my own experience and how I choose to live my life. Other musicians may have a different account of their day-to-day life, and the show routine can potentially be different.

If you are a working theatre musician, please share your stories and comments on showmusician.com and on facebook.com/showmusician.com

9

Equipment

Having reliable and good-sounding equipment is extremely important as a professional musician. Not only do you need to have high-quality equipment but also the right equipment for the job. Depending on the show, you will need to have equipment that can recreate the sounds needed for the show, whether it's to represent the genre of music or to produce what the composer intended in the score. Sometimes you will get a brief about what instrument you will need to bring. If this is very specific, often the producer will provide the instruments for you. More often than not, you will need to make your own judgement on what to bring, especially for guitars and drums, so make sure you research the music well beforehand to find out what will give you the sound you need.

KEYBOARDS

On large scale shows it is customary that all keyboards are provided by the company, since they are often specific to the show and the sounds needed. They will in most cases also be

Equipment

programmed specifically for the show by a keyboard programmer. The keyboard programmer will most often be on hand at the initial band call to make any adjustments and help with keyboard-related issues. On commercial shows you will in most cases not be responsible for the programming of any sounds on your instrument or fixing any issues, unless they are very basic. The keyboard programmer will be called in to fix any problems or to alter any sounds or programming. If you notice any issues, make sure you report them straight away to your MD. On lower budget shows it's unlikely that a keyboard programmer will be hired in, so you will generally need to provide your own keyboards and be in charge of any keyboard-related issues. For these shows it would be good practise to get to know your instrument well, what sounds it has to offer, and how to do basic programming.

GUITARS

When making a decision on what equipment to use for each show, you need first of all to find out the specification for the show and if any specific guitars are needed. If not, make a musical judgement depending on the musical style and genre. You need to be as authentic to the style as possible, even if you need go out and purchase another instrument (remember it's all tax-deductible). You need to know if you can use an amplifier or not, and make sure that you find out if you need any specific effects. On occasion, guitars will be provided by the company, especially if the band is visible or if a specific sound is needed. Examples of shows where guitars are provided are *We Will Rock You*, for that Bryan May sound, and *Jersey Boys*, where an authentic period look and sound is needed.

Guitar Effects

Unlike the keyboard programmer, the guitarist is usually left to program in the sounds needed for the show, but again there are exceptions like *We Will Rock You*, where guitar effects are provided. Try to get hold of the pad and a recording of the show well before the first band call so that you can program in as many of the sounds as you need. This will save you loads of time in the band calls so that you can concentrate on playing and not be constantly stressing about finding that next sound. Inevitably, changes will need to be made in the band calls, but having the general sounds programmed beforehand will make your life much easier. Make sure that you are familiar with the latest guitar effects being used and how to use them. Line 6 and Fractal Audio effects are commonly used digital guitar effects at the time of writing.

DRUMS

Make sure that you have at least one good-quality drum kit that is versatile for different scenarios and musical styles. If you have the facility to have a few different kits for different applications, great, but often the ability to purchase numerous drum kits and the ease to store them when they are not in use can be difficult. You need to have a good understanding of how different styles of music will require different tuning of the drums and the use of different drum heads. You will also need a variety of different cymbals and snare drums. Musical theatre has many varieties of musical styles, so you need to

Equipment

have cymbals that suit both rock and jazz and everything in between. Again, having cymbals that are versatile is a good idea, since you can play many different styles of music in a show and will not have time to swap cymbals during a performance — the same goes for snare drums and the kit as a whole. So when you purchase your equipment, bear this in mind and try to choose equipment that will work with most applications. As an example, make sure you don't just have a kit with big rock-size drums or smaller jazz-size drums. Have something that is more general and versatile. Get to know your equipment well, how to tune your drums for different styles, and what drum heads work best for what sound on your kit. When you arrive at the first band call and sound check, it is important that you can get a good and appropriate sound quickly, since time is often very limited.

Electronic Setup: V-drums

It's good to own some basic electronics like an Octapad, V-drums, or something similar. Know how to program them and how to plug them into a PA system. Borrow one from a friend if you can't afford to purchase one to familiarise yourself with the technology.

Basic Percussion and Pantomime Essentials

Make sure you own basic percussion equipment, mark tree, cowbell, wood blocks, triangle, bell tree, shaker, mountable tambourine, and learn how to play them musically.

For pantomimes you'll need, as well as the above, duck call, swanee whistle (slide whistle), kazoo, siren whistle, vibraslap, and more.

Percussion

A percussion setup can be extremely varied, depending on the show, so make sure that you find out well in advance what you'll need. It is usually expected that a percussionist will own all the essential equipment and will provide them, including timpani, xylophone, vibraphone, and congas, but on occasion some of the bigger instruments will be provided by the show. Make sure that you check about transport and protection for your instrument well in advance, if you're touring. Any unusual instruments needed for the show will usually be provided or at least compensated for if you have to buy them specifically.

Front Line, Strings, and Specialist Instruments

Front line, which includes any brass and woodwind instruments, are of course very personal instruments and will therefore always be provided by the player. Again, make sure that you are aware of all the parts you may need to cover and if there are any unusual instruments you may need to play. Maintain your instrument well, have it serviced regularly, and make sure that you have necessary spares on hand. Tuning your instrument to the piano being used on the show can be useful and then also as a section before the show starts.

Equipment Maintenance

It is extremely important to have with you any spares that you may need for your instrument. If anything should go wrong with your instrument, you need to be able to get it fixed as

Equipment

quickly as possible to minimise any disruption to the show. Of course, make sure that you have the obvious spares, like picks and strings for guitars, sticks and heads for drums, and reeds for wind instruments, but also think about how crucial your instrument is in the show. For example, if you have many solo lines that are crucial to the flow of the show, it may also be a good idea to have a spare instrument on hand so that you can change quickly in an emergency.

Note

If you are bringing your own electrical equipment, sometimes the company will request that it is PAT tested for safety. PAT stands for Portable Appliance Testing and can be carried out by most electricians. This can include anything that needs to be plugged into an electrical mains socket. Check if this is needed before your first call.

Guitarists

Bring a spare guitar of a similar type and sound that you use the most in the show and make sure that you also tune it before the show.

Drummers

Bring a spare snare drum and have it close by in case your main one breaks or the head goes. Also, remember to have spare drum heads with you, including a bass drum head, just in case. If you're a heavy player, having a spare bass drum pedal may also be a good idea. Make sure you let the fixer and the sound designer know about your setup well in advance, especially if you happen to use an unusual setup. For instance, if you use four or five toms as standard, it might be a good idea to let the sound designer know so that they can make the necessary preparations.

Tip

Just remember to keep your spares close by and also make sure that you keep your instrument in good working order. Check that everything is working as it should well before the show. Don't just sit down two minutes before the show starts and expect everything to be okay. Give yourself enough time to get things fixed if there is a problem. This also goes for instruments that are provided by the show, like keyboards. Check that everything is working well before the show starts.

INSTRUMENT ENDORSEMENT DEALS

If you are on a relatively big show and have a reasonably decent CV/resume, it might be worth trying to get some endorsement deals with your instrument manufacturer. This is particularly useful for breakables like strings, reeds, drumsticks, and heads and can save you a fair amount of money over the time you are working on a show. You will

Equipment

also usually be able to keep your endorsement deal after the show is finished and can carry on getting your products at a reduced cost for years to come.

Most companies will offer some sort of an artist deal, which is usually about a third of the retail price. Contact the company distributor in your country or area to find out what they can offer you. They will usually have an artist relations person you can deal with directly. They may ask in exchange if they can have a mention in the program for the show and may ask for you to be involved in some publicity if need be. You will need to speak to your fixer and company manager well before the show starts about putting things in the program, since programs will usually be printed well in advance.

If you are on a high-publicity show or in the West End or Broadway, many companies will consider providing equipment on loan for the duration of the show free of charge. This is common for drum equipment and sometimes keyboards and guitars. Again, this will have to be addressed far in advance and will need to be cleared with the fixer, musical supervisor, the company manager, and even the producers. So get the ball rolling early if you want to explore this option, if it hasn't been sorted out already by the producers.

10

The Unions

What are the unions for, and do you need to be in one? The answer is a little complex and does depend on which side of the Atlantic you live, but I'll try to explain as best I can. Please note that this only applies to working in the UK or the US, so if you live elsewhere, please check your local union for information in your area. In Chapter 4 we talked about the different union contracts in the UK and the US and some of the many rates of pay and extras that you might encounter. In this chapter I'm going to give you some more information on how the unions are structured, some of the organisations that are connected to the unions, and the cost of being a member.

What Do the Unions Do?

The unions are a trade union body that represent their members and negotiate working terms and conditions on their behalf, as well as assisting in any work-related issues with regards to employment law, contracts, and other legal matters. They also provide advice and assistance to members on numerous issues related to the industry. In basic terms, the unions make sure that musicians are not exploited by their employers. They help put into place a legal framework of pay, holiday, travel, sick pay, and other aspects related to fair and transparent pay structure for musicians. If the unions were not there, employers could get away with offering musicians the national minimum wage, which is far lower than the minimum wage negotiated by the unions. But for all this to apply, you have to have signed a union contract with your employer.

The biggest difference between the UK Musicians' Union and the American Union, AFM, is that in the UK you don't have to be in the union to work. You can accept a job, whether it's a union contract or not, and you legally accept the terms in the contract that you sign. The chance is, though, if you have signed a union contract, the rate of pay will be higher, since the employer will have to comply with the union-agreed rates of pay and benefits.

In the States, to work on Broadway you have to be in the Union, Local 802, and that also means you cannot accept any work that is not union-approved. This is often referred to as a 'closed shop'; only union members can take on union-agreed work.

Lets have a look at the unions on both sides of the Atlantic.

THE MUSICIANS' UNION - UK

The MU (Musicians' Union) is the union body in the UK and has six regional offices and an executive committee of elected members. It also has a number of Sections and Section

Committees that cover the different areas of a musician's work and which MU members can join.

As mentioned before, there are two union contracts that you are most likely to come across when working in theatre. In the West End of London there is the SOLT agreement, and outside of London there is the UKT agreement, formally known as the TMA (Theatrical Management Association) agreement.

Society of London Theatres (SOLT)

The SOLT agreement is connected to certain theatres in London, which is classed as the West End. If you work in a theatre in London and it's not part of the SOLT group of theatres, you will not be on a SOLT agreement. The SOLT rates of pay are higher than the UKT rates but do not include things like touring allowance or travel as extras, because it is assumed that musicians working in London also live in London, or at least the surrounding area. There are, however, some extras paid for doubling on instruments and holiday pay, which is covered in more detail in Chapter 4, 'Working in Musical Theatre.'

United Kingdom Theatre (UKT)

The UKT contract applies to theatres outside of London's SOLT theatres and relates to touring and regional productions. The basic pay is less than the SOLT agreement but has extras like touring allowance and travel added, since musicians on these productions will be working away from home and will need to book digs (accommodation) and pay for travel expenses. (See the 'Touring' chapter for more information.)

THE AMERICAN FEDERATION OF MUSICIANS - USA

The AFM (American Federation of Musicians) is the union body in the States and Canada. The AFM is made up of more than 250 local unions throughout the United States and Canada and is the largest organisation in the world representing the interests of professional musicians. The AFM follows a code of conduct referred to as Bylaws. You can read the AFM Bylaws on its website (see below).

Just like in the UK, there are different agreements for musicians on Broadway and touring musicians. The AFM Pamphlet B Touring Agreement covers musicians travelling with theatrical productions in the United States and Canada, and the Broadway CBA Agreement covers musicians working on Broadway. Both the Pamphlet B and Broadway CBAs are agreements with the Broadway League of Theatre Owners and Producers. Within the Pamphlet B agreement there is also a separate contract for smaller, shorter-stay productions, which is called the Short Engagement Tour Agreement (SET) and allows lower rates for musicians on these often lower-budget tours. There are also other organisations in the US that represent the interests of theatre musicians, like the TMA.

The TMA

The TMA (Theatre Musicians Association) is a non-profit organisation representing theatre musicians in the US and Canada and has offices in many major cities across the United

States, referred to as chapters. The TMA serves as an information network between theatre musicians and the union, and among theatre musicians themselves, both on tour, on Broadway, and other cities across the US and Canada.

The Broadway Theatre Committee

The Broadway Theatre Committee is similar to the TMA in many ways but represents musicians in Local 802, which is the local for New York City and Broadway.

Local 802, Broadway, New York City

Broadway musicians are covered by the Broadway CBA Agreement, and to work on a Broadway show you have to be in the union, the Local 802. On Broadway the union enforces a minimum numbers rule, which insists that certain number of musicians be employed by each theatre. This number is dependent on the size of theatre, so the bigger the theatre, the more musicians need to be employed. This number has decreased over the years, with the producers continuing to try to get the numbers down. When a production only needs a smaller amount of musicians because of the nature of the show, for instance when the band is on stage, an agreement is often made with union to allow this to happen. More details can be found in the CBA agreement.

The Broadway League

Another organisation worth mentioning is the Broadway League, which is the national trade association for the Broadway industry. It has over 700 members, including theatre owners and operators, producers, presenters, and general managers in North American cities. The organisation's mission includes serving the various needs of theatrical producers in New York and of national touring shows, as well as presenters of touring productions in cities throughout North America. The Broadway League and Disney Theatricals are the main employers of touring shows in the US and are signed to the AFM's Pamphlet B Agreement and the Short Engagement Tour (SET) Agreement mentioned above. The AFM has to negotiate with the League when trying to secure better terms for theatre musicians in the US.

OTHER UNION BENEFITS

As we talked about in Chapter 4, the unions also offer many other services to their members, as well as negotiating rates of pay. This includes public liability insurance, free or discounted instrument insurance, free legal help in any dispute over pay or working conditions, and advice on any issue related to your employment as a musician in or outside theatre. You also get put on the national list of union musicians, where you can be found by other union members for work in your area. One of the most important reasons to be in the union, and to support the union, is that as a collective of thousands of musicians, the unions have the power to negotiate and influence the employment conditions and standards of musicians across the industry. Without the power of the unions, the rates of pay and the future of the musician, both in theatre and in other industries, will deteriorate as producers and other employers will try to enforce a lower rate of pay and longer working hours.

How Much Does it Cost to be in the Union?

In the UK the cost for a yearly membership is at the time of writing £207, or £213 if paid in installments. If you are a student, a membership is just £20.

In the US it's $220 for the year to join Local 802 Broadway. Check your local union for rates in your area.

The TMA dues are $40 for the year.

UNION WEBSITES

The Musicians' Union in the UK

www.musiciansunion.org.uk

UK Theatre

www.uktheatre.org

The American Federation of Musicians in North America

www.afm.org

Theater Musicians Association in North America

www.afm-tma.org

11

Touring

Touring is something that most musicians will need to do at some point in their career. The state of the industry today dictates that there just aren't enough local gigs for everyone. Tours can take on many forms. There are the long-running international tours that will travel the world and stay for a few weeks or months in each city. There are the shorter international tours that only do a few weeks or even days in a city and then move on, although these are normally a part of a national tour that will just do the foreign venue as a part of the touring schedule. The most common are the national tours. These will travel the country and do one night in each town (one-nighter tour) or more commonly do a week (weekly tours), two weeks, or even months in each town. How long a show stays in each town depends on the size of the show, how much the producers feel that it will sell, and possibly other factors like theatre availability. Also, some shows have huge sets, so the get-in for the show can take a long time, which means that the show may stay longer in each venue.

THE TOURING PROCESS

As with shows in the West End and on Broadway, there is a production period for touring shows, but it can often be shorter. Rehearsals for a touring show can either happen somewhere like London or New York City (basically where it's easy for the creatives to get to), and then the production period or technical rehearsals will happen in the theatre of the first touring venue. On occasion the rehearsals do take place in the same town as the first touring venue or can be split between two towns like London and the first touring city. It just depends on what works best for getting the show up and running as quickly as possible.

The MD and assistant MD will always be in for the entire rehearsal period and sometimes the drummer, and possibly also the bass player for the last week or two. The first time the whole band will get together is most often on the first day of technical rehearsals in the first touring venue. The exception to this is when it's a new show being performed for the first time, or rewritten; then there is sometimes a band rehearsal period prior to the technical week.

As explained previously, after the initial band calls, pit setup, sound checks, and dress rehearsals, the show enters its normal running period. So at the end of the last show of the first venue, which can be a weekly, fortnightly or longer, you need to pack up your gear to either take with you to the next venue or to put on the trucks for transporting along with the rest of the set and other show equipment.

Touring

You need to check in advance with the technical and production team how much space you will have available on the trucks for your instrument and what flight cases or otherwise are provided, if any. This is especially important if you play a bulky instrument like percussion, drums, or double bass, but things like guitar amps also need to be checked out. If you have a bulky instrument or equipment that will take up room, I would speak to the fixer before the first band call to try to figure out what will be provided for transport. The production company will often provide some flight cases that the band can use and will normally expect to have to transport things like drum kits and percussion equipment on the trucks, but it is still worth double-checking this. What you don't want is to assume that cases are provided and space allocated for your instrument, only to find out late on a Saturday night that there are no cases or space on the trucks, and you need to transport everything with you to the next venue. So make sure you address this early on so that there is enough time to get things sorted out.

Tip

Always be polite and understanding when dealing with the production, stage management, and sound teams. They are very busy on get-in and get-out days and need to get a lot done in a very short time, so don't expect them to be at your beck and call. If you treat them with respect, they will be much more helpful to you in return.

The get-in

You've now done the first venue and your first get-out, and you arrive at venue number two on the tour. Depending on the show, you will most likely start either on a Monday or Tuesday, although some of the bigger shows can start later in the week to allow more time to get the stage set up. You will have had a schedule from the fixer, and also possibly the company manager, about start times for each venue. The sound check time should now have been set and will be the same for every get-in day at the start of each venue.

> **Note**
>
> Sometimes on a new show the sound check and setup times can get changed as you get into the tour, since the production team might not be entirely sure at the start how long everything is going to take to get set up. So they may give a setup time that is slightly earlier than needed just in case they need the extra time. This is changed to later in the day when things have been sorted out and the get-in is smoother.

The band get-in is usually scheduled for the afternoon before the first performance. You can expect to be called for a 'seating call' anywhere from 1:00 p.m. to 5:00 p.m., depending on the show. A seating call is an allocated time slot before the sound check when you need to be in the pit. When the actual sound check time arrives, you need to be ready to play, which means that you will have set up all your equipment, checked that it works, checked your monitor mix, and tuned your instrument.

The larger instruments that take longer to set up, like drums and percussion, will often be called earlier than the rest of the band to give them time to set up. You will in most cases be paid extra for this time, but it is becoming more common that this time is part of a three-hour call that includes the setup and sound check. If you have no allocated seating call or setup time in your schedule, make sure that you allow enough time to get your instrument set up and ready to play for the allocated sound check times.

> **Note**
>
> Make sure that you check your contract carefully with regards to what time you get paid for your setup time and sound check. If it looks unreasonable or unclear, ask for clarification, especially if you have a long setup time, which will overrun any arranged call time. For example, the UKT agreement allows for an overtime payment if it takes you longer than fifteen minutes to set up your equipment.

The Sound check

What happens in the sound check? The sound department should already have done a line check to make sure that all microphones and cables are working. They then do a quick sound check of each instrument, most often starting with the drums. When each instrument has done its check, the band will play together something from the show, like the overture or a piece where everyone in the band is playing. It is common to have to play the same piece a few times while the sound department adjusts the sound in the auditorium. The length of the sound check for the band does vary between shows from fifteen minutes to an hour, but it is usually on the shorter side.

After the band has done its sound check and played a few pieces from the show, the singers are brought on stage and their microphones are tested; however, this is sometimes done prior to the band sound check. When they are all ready, the band will play a few numbers from the show, this time with the singers. Normally there will be a set schedule for the sound check that lists what songs get played; this will include music from the show that has the whole ensemble singing, and then each of the songs that feature a lead vocal. This is done so that the performers can make sure they can hear everything that they need on stage, ready for the performance in the evening.

When everyone is happy or time runs out, the sound check is done. The musicians are paid per a three-hour call, and the producers do not want that call to run over, since they will then have to pay every musician in the band overtime payment. It is common practise that when the allocated call is up, the musicians are broken and are allowed to leave, but the sound check carries on onstage with the vocals and the MD staying on. The MD and the singers are often on a buyout for the sound check and technical rehearsals, so the producer does not have to pay them any extra if it runs over.

On the more technically complex shows, it is common for a technical rehearsal to follow the sound check. This can sometimes continue until less than an hour before the start of the performance. The get-in days can be extremely busy and hectic for the stage management team, who will have been in the theatre since early hours, and sometimes overnight to get everything set up. There is a lot that needs to be done to get a show up and ready. Everything gets toured between venues: sound, lighting and staging, down to the floor. It is a complex puzzle to put together at times and with minimal time allocated. We, the musicians, are only one part in this huge scenario.

After the sound check, there is normally a break of about an hour or two before the performance to grab some food and possibly check into your digs. After that first manic day, the show is up and running, and for us musicians it is into the standard show week.

THE UKT AGREEMENT (UK TOURING)

In the UK, when you sign a union contract you will be following the guidelines of the UKT agreement (United Kingdom Theatre). We looked at some of the elements of this agreement in Chapter 4, and the rates of pay you can expect. The UKT states many of guidelines that producers will need to follow when it comes to paying you touring allowances and other fees associated with touring. Your pay will usually be split into the following categories:

Basic pay: This is your payment for playing eight shows a week, or however many you have been contracted to do.

Overtime and extras: This is any overtime that you might have incurred and any extra calls like rehearsals or extra shows that you might have done.

Touring allowance: This is what you get paid for staying away from home, including digs (accommodation) and food.

Travel: This is your travel expenses from venue to venue or from your home to the venue.

Let's look at this in more detail.

TRAVEL

Travelling is something you will be doing a lot of when touring, as you would expect. You need to be extremely organised and need to plan well in advance. As mentioned above, you get paid the travel cost from venue to venue or from your home to venue. How this works, for example, if at the start of a tour you will be travelling from your home address to the first venue of the tour, it is assumed that you stay on tour, so you will then be paid travel from that first venue to the second, and so on. This goes on until there is a break in the tour schedule and a holiday week is confirmed. You will then be paid travel from the last venue before the holiday week to your home address. Then you will be paid travel from your home address to the next venue on the tour after the holiday week. When the tour finishes, you will be paid travel to your home address again.

Touring

At the start of the tour you will need to decide what mode of transport you want to be paid for. The options in the UKT agreement are to be paid per mile or a train fare. You will need to make this option at the start of the contract and then stick to it; you cannot swap and change once the tour has started. At the time of writing, the agreement states that 26 pence is payable per mile travelled, and a standard rail fare is payable, which can be booked up to two weeks before travel date. The mileage is calculated using the shortest route possible.

Note

Just because you chose, for example, mileage payment at the start of the tour, that does not mean you have to travel by car everywhere and that you can't use the train or fly. It just means that it will be the method used to calculate the money you will receive for travel expenses each time you travel.

Pros and Cons of Car Versus Train

Which is the best method to choose and what works out better financially? This can be a difficult decision, and there is often very little in the difference between what you get paid in mileage and in train fare. Some musicians are convinced that rail fare is the better option, while others think mileage. What you can do to get some idea is look at your touring schedule and then work out a comparison on a spreadsheet, calculating the mileage between each venue and the cost using the current rate per mile and then the same journeys using a rail fare, booked two weeks before the travel date. The resources to use for this are Google Maps for calculating the mileage and any rail ticket purchasing site like National Rail or The Trainline. To calculate the mileage, use the actual venue as the start and end points, and not your digs or the city centre.

From this you should be able to get a general idea of which travel method will be better financially. Remember that this is just to determine the better choice when it comes to the producers calculating your travel payment and has nothing to do with which travel method you use. You can easily travel by car to some venues and by train or plane to another. Just look at each venue independently and decide which mode of transport works best. For instance, if you are travelling to a city with a six-hour drive, then considering flying there makes sense. Just bear in mind the extra time and cost involved getting to and from the airport on each side of your journey.

Note

You have to consider that when travelling by rail or flying, there is hardly ever a train or plane late enough in the evening to get you home or to the next venue directly after the show. This means you will need to stay another night and travel the next morning. And of course it means having to spend another night in accommodation, which is more expense if you are paying per night. Plus you will be missing out on a night at home, if you are heading home between venues.

Parking

There is much to organise when it comes to travelling on tour. You of course have to allocate plenty of time to get there and allow for traffic disruptions and breaks along the way. If driving, you must also consider parking. Parking in city centres can be difficult and very expensive, so make sure that you look into it BEFORE you get there. Otherwise you can be badly stung by a hefty parking bill. You most often won't have any time to try to figure out which carpark is the cheapest when you arrive in a city when the sound check start time is getting ever closer.

So here are a few parking tips:

- Check with the theatre whether they have any parking deals with local carparks. They may even have some parking available at the theatre.
- Check whether your digs or hotel has any free parking.
- Use online tools to check out car parking in the city before you get there. Parkopedia is a good resource.
- Check out resources from which you can rent parking spaces, just make sure they are secure; justpark.com, yourparkingspace.co.uk, and parklet.co.uk are good

UK resources. Do an Internet search for similar services in your area.

- Ask other members of the band for recommendations.

- See if there are possibly any residential roads with free parking within a walk or a bus ride. You can then leave the car there for the week if you don't need use of it.

- Check out whether there are any park-and-ride facilities, which are cheaper, especially if you are commuting in. Note that you can rarely leave your car overnight in a Park & Ride in the UK, although weekly passes are sometimes available. Check the websites for details.

Often there is free parking in the evenings, so time your travel so that you get there just before the free period starts. It can often get busy when the free parking period starts, so if you get there a bit before and pay for just thirty minutes or an hour, you are more likely to get a space.

If you are commuting and have an afternoon show, park your car in a free residential road and then pick it up between shows and move it nearer the theatre for a quick getaway after the show, providing there is free or cheap parking available in the evening.

Make sure that you park your car somewhere reasonably secure. The last thing you want is to find your car vandalised or stolen at the end of the week, when all you want to do is to get home. In a foreign city it can be difficult to know what is a safe area, so ask around. The stage door staff at the theatres are often good people to ask, or the more experienced members of the band who have toured for a long time.

SUBSISTENCE

Subsistence is the part of your touring allowance that includes things like food, drink, and basically anything you need to survive on tour. What is the best way to survive on tour without spending a fortune? This comes down to a few factors, your personal preference of food and drink, as well as what accommodation you stay in. If you have accommodation where you can cook, you can most likely eat more cheaply than eating out in restaurants every day, unless you buy prime steaks and lobster to cook, of course. If you stay frequently in self-catering accommodation, it's a good idea to have a box of essential cooking and kitchen items in the boot of your car. This will save you having to buy the same basics every time you get to a new town, and the accommodation does not provide them. You can also tour things like coffee-making equipment, blenders, etc., depending on your eating habits.

If you prefer to eat out, or you usually stay in hotels and places where you can't cook, it's still possible to eat well and affordably on tour — you just have to know where to go and a few money-saving tips. Town centres offer a much bigger variety of food than they used to, and healthy food is becoming more accessible. When eating out every day, it can be very easy to just reach for the quick and cheap option like McDonald's or something similar. Just bear in mind that eating food like that every day will start to take its toll very quickly on your health and wellbeing.

Breakfast

If you stay in a hotel, you can bring some supplies with you and eat in your hotel room for breakfast, if it isn't included in your hotel booking. Pick up some fruit and some porridge pots that only need hot water to prepare. The majority of hotels have a kettle in the room, so you can make yourself breakfast in the mornings without the need for storing any milk.

Lunch

Most coffee shops will offer things like sandwiches and toast and salads that you can have with a coffee for lunch. The coffee shop culture is also handy for us touring lot, since it's somewhere we can hang out before we have to go to work, saving us from staying in our hotel room all day long. Use Google to find good recommended coffee shops in each town so that you don't have to rely on the coffee chains every time — this is especially helpful if you're into good coffee.

Evening Meal

There is usually a huge variety of choice in restaurants in most big cities. So that you are not spending a fortune, and to limit the choice a little, check out the discount websites and apps that offer discounts in well-known restaurants. You can also join dining clubs that offer similar deals. By using these deals, you can eat extremely well without spending a fortune on meals, often in very good restaurants. In the UK check out sites like Vouchercloud, Vouchercodes, and dining clubs like Taste. I'm sure there are many more. Most of them will also have apps for your phone, which makes it easy to find places. Wherever in the world you happen to be touring, use the Internet to locate good restaurants and deals.

If restaurants are not your thing, or you just need a little variety, you can also get a decent meal from most supermarkets in the way of ready-made salads, sandwiches, or ready meals that you can pick up and eat back at your digs or in the theatre dressing room. Whatever you do, just make sure that you are eating a healthy and balanced diet, since this can very easily be forgotten on tour.

DIGS

One of the most important things to organise when you're touring is accommodation or digs. Your touring allowance is not massive, so you have to be resourceful in how you book accommodation without spending a fortune. There are numerous ways to find affordable accommodation, and I will go through some of the more common resources. You can of course use a mixture of these, and there are always new resources becoming available online to make the process easier. The traditional way for people working in the theatre to find accommodation is through the digs lists.

Digs Lists

Each major theatre in the UK has available to anyone who is working at the theatre a list of accommodation in the area. This is a list that consists of commercial accommodation like hotels, bed & breakfast, hostels, self-catering flats and houses, and also noncommercial accommodation, which is essentially rooms for hire in people's private houses. The people that offer rooms in their houses are often associated with the theatre in some way and offer people who are working at the theatre an affordable place to stay. This is a way for them to make a little extra money on their spare room in their house, and they can charge as little as £50 a week for a room, although this is now becoming rare, and £80 to £150+ a week is more common.

The problem with private digs is that you often have no idea what the standard of the accommodation is like until you get there. There are often no reviews or photographs available of the accommodation, so it can be a bit of a gamble. In many cases the accommodation is absolutely fine, as long as you are comfortable with staying in a stranger's house. However, sometimes the accommodation is seriously substandard and is somewhere you will not feel comfortable staying. This has happened to me a number of times, and it can be an awkward situation when you have to make your excuses and leave. Plus it can cause you real problems, since you have no other accommodation booked, and you need to find somewhere else last-minute, which can be costly. So the plus side of theatre digs lists is that you can often find reasonably cheap accommodation, and if you're lucky it can also be a nice place to stay.

If you decide to use the Theatre Digs List, here are a few tips:

- Get recommendations from people you know that have stayed there before.

Touring

- Call the digs directly and ask questions about the things that are important to you. Does it have a shower, can I use the kitchen? etc.
- If it's a commercial place, check it out online.

Bear in mind that people's idea of nice accommodation can vary greatly. Some people's standards are much lower than others, and some people are happy to put up with things that you wouldn't.

To get hold of a theatre digs list, you can either contact each theatre directly, and they will most likely email one to you, or speak to your company manager, who often has them on file. Many of the digs that are on the digs lists have now been made available online and include both photos and reviews. See below for more information.

Hotel chains can also offer reasonable deals, if you book well enough in advance, and there are now many online tools from which you can book private accommodation where reviews and photos are provided, like Airbnb and others (see list below of resources). Another option that is becoming more popular is to use Facebook. You can just search for theatre digs, and there are numerous groups where you can literally list the town and dates that you need digs for, and people will then get back to you with recommendations or offers of accommodation from your requests. This can clearly be extremely convenient and useful, but again do your research well before committing. Ask the necessary questions about the accommodation and ask for photographs to be emailed to you.

If there is the possibility of sharing accommodation with a few people that you work with, a good option is to rent out a flat or a house for the time you need. You will of course have your own bedroom but would share the living space with a few others. This option is one of my favourites, since you can have a place to yourself (i.e., not with the owner living with you) and have access to a kitchen and a living space. This can also reduce living costs, since you can cook and make food at the digs, thus reducing the cost of eating out every meal, as you would if you were staying in a hotel. If sharing is not an option, or you would rather have your private space, a hotel is probably your best bet. For finding self-catering accommodation, you can check out the theatre digs list, which sometimes has a few on there, or just Google 'Self Catering Accommodation' in the city you are travelling to. Some of the resources listed below will also have self-catering listed.

Note

With self-catering accommodation, and some hotels and other accommodation, you may need to pay a deposit to secure the booking, and you may even need to pay the full amount before you arrive, often weeks before. If you are sharing, the easiest way to deal with this is for whoever is making the booking to pay, and then collect the money from the other parties. Just make sure that you inform the other parties that this is happening and get the money off them as soon as possible.

Touring

I will usually book my accommodation in the following way: I will go through the tour schedule as soon as I get it. This is even before the first band call has happened. I will check whether any of the venues have digs that I have used before, and I know and trust. I will then go ahead and book those as soon as possible.

Be careful when booking digs with hotels or anywhere where you may have to pay up-front, or if there is no cancellation option. The producers can, and often do, change the tour schedule even after the first schedule has been sent out to the cast, crew, and musicians. Also, some tours will not last the course and can be pulled before the end. Any accommodation that you have booked without an option to cancel will be at your loss. You need to make a judgement about the tour that you are doing on how secure it is. I will always go directly to the theatre website in each venue to double-check that the show is advertised and that tickets are being offered for sale before I even consider booking any nonrefundable accommodation. If you have any concerns about whether the show might run its course, if some of the venues on the touring schedule have not yet been confirmed, or are not advertised on the theatre's website, wait until a little closer to the time to book anything nonrefundable. Be particularly wary if you are on a lower-budget show and a show that is either new and untested or has a reputation of not selling well in the past.

Tip

Always go directly to the theatre website in each venue to double-check that the show is advertised and that tickets are being offered for sale before you book any nonrefundable accommodation. Also, check the start day. Some venues may start on a Tuesday and not the normal Monday, for example.

If I'm happy that the tour schedule is reasonably secure, and I have done all the possible checks, I will go ahead and book as many digs as I can, at least for the first few months of the tour. If you have friends on the tour, it might be worth getting in touch and seeing if they would like to possibly share some accommodation.

Tip

It is usually not worth trying to share with more than two other people when booking digs, since finding more than three-bedroom accommodation can be difficult.

If you don't know anyone to share with, make sure that you book at least the first couple of venues. You can then see if there is anyone you can share with after you get to meet and know some of the people on the tour. If you'd rather just have your own space and not have to rely on others to share, then go ahead and book some digs. If sharing, it is worth searching the Internet for agencies that deal in Self Catering Accommodation, as mention earlier. This is especially useful in the more touristy towns.

In the UK I will normally start with the hotel chains and the theatre digs websites. I will do this in order of standard, starting with the highest, and then compare prices.

Tip

Some hotel chains will not appear on comparison websites like booking.com, so you will need to go directly to their website. Premier Inn and Travelodge are two well-known UK hotel chains this applies to.

I will open up a few tabs in my browser and connect to the following sites:

- Premier Inn
- Ibis
- Travelodge
- booking.com
- theatredigsbooker

I will then put in the dates for the first venue I need to book in each of the websites and see how they compare. I will also have a map open so that I can see where the hotel is in relation to the theatre. You also must take into consideration parking if you're driving, and if you're on the train or flying, you will need an extra night stay, as explained before. Have a budget in mind for each venue and try to stick to it. You will, however, have to bear in mind that some towns will always be more expensive than others, if they are big tourist places and depending on the time of year, so alter your budget accordingly.

If all these results turn out to be too expensive, I would try one of the other resources like Airbnb, some of the other theatre digs list websites, and Facebook. If everything turns to be out of budget, you have a couple of options. Either increase your budget a little or consider booking digs farther out and then commuting in. You could book something that is on a good bus route, is an easy drive in (if there is some affordable parking near the theatre), or is on a train line that is not too far or expensive; just make sure there is public transport going back late enough to get you back after the show.

Booking digs can be a very time-consuming exercise, since there are many factors that you need to consider. It is, however, worth taking the time to get it right, since having good and convenient digs can make the touring life a lot more enjoyable, while bad digs can make it an awful experience. The more touring you do, the more you'll get to know each town and where is good to stay. You will also come to learn how you choose to live your life on tour, and whether you prefer hotels, self-catering, or private digs, or a combination.

In some venues you can even check out the holiday parks for caravans or camping, if that is something you are comfortable with. Just bear in mind that camping might be romantic and adventurous for a night or two but may be not for a whole week or two.

The way we book digs is ever changing, and with social media it's becoming an even easier task than it used to be. Hopefully by using the tools listed here and some of the advice given, you can make booking digs an easy and painless experience.

ACCOMMODATION ONLINE BOOKING TOOLS

General Accommodation

- booking.com
- travelodge.co.uk
- premierinn.co.uk
- laterooms.co.uk
- traveladvisor.co.uk
- ibis.co.uk
- airbnb.com

Theatre-Specific

- theatredigsbooker.com
- Facebook - search 'theatre digs'

- theatredigs.co.uk
- showdigs.co.uk

Self-Catering

- Check Google for local self-catering agencies and websites
- Airbnb and select the entire home option
- Holiday lettings
- booking.com has some self-catering listed.

Note

If your home address is within twenty-five miles of the venue, no touring allowance will be paid.

FOREIGN/INTERNATIONAL VENUES

If you're on a tour that travels outside your home country, slightly different rules apply. You will no longer receive your touring allowance but will instead get some spending money, which is referred to as 'per diems.' This is a daily amount that you will normally get in cash on the first day of the foreign venue, in the local currency. Commonly, a week will be paid out in advance. In the UK the UKT contract includes this amount in the currency for most countries around the world.

The producers do have an option of providing meals for the company, and the per diems will be decreased in relation to how many meals they provide. The UKT agreement explains how this works in more detail. If the producers decide to go this route, make sure you let them know of any dietary requirements well in advance.

When working abroad, the accommodation is also booked for you. There are the occasional exceptions to this rule, but that is rare. If accommodation is not booked for you, make sure that you receive an adequate amount of travel allowance to cover the cost of a hotel in the town you will be staying, taking into consideration local taxes that can be added and any other expenses involved. It is normal procedure that the producer will book any accommodation and travel for you. This will include travel to and from airports (in the foreign country only), flights, ferries, and trains, a good-quality hotel or serviced apartment, and any travel costs to and from the accommodation and the venue. You will not be expected to share a bedroom with anyone, although you may need to share an apartment if they have more than one bedroom.

Note

When touring in the UK, the Republic of Ireland does get classed as an abroad venue, so the same rules apply. Northern Ireland does, however, not get classed as a foreign venue, so the same rules as on mainland UK apply.

When working in some countries in Europe, you may find that some tax will be taken off your pay each week. Germany is one such country. This is a withholding tax from the local government, which you can then claim back at a later date. Speak to your company manager about this and how this will work in whatever country you are in.

ORGANISATION

When touring, you need to be very organised and plan well in advance. You need to book digs and flights early to get the cheapest deals, and you need to be aware of travelling times and distances so that you always get to each venue in plenty of time.

Having an organised diary is very important, and I recommend using a digital diary that backs up automatically and can alert you of important dates and things to do. Apple's iCal and Google's diary both do this as well, as well as many other third-party software solutions; find the one that works for you and is reliable.

Keeping track of expenses is also crucial both for your own finances and for tax purposes. Make sure that you have a system of tracking your expenses while on tour so that you can claim everything possible on your tax return at the end of the tax year. I try to pay as much as possible on debit or credit cards, since you then have a record of every transaction you have done. If you pay with cash, make sure that you keep all receipts for your records. I go into this in more detail in the 'Self-Employment' chapter.

If you drive, make sure that you keep your vehicle in good condition and have it serviced and checked regularly. I would recommend investing in a good and reliable vehicle if you are planning on touring for a while, since having car issues en route to a venue can be highly inconvenient and extremely stressful. Remember, there are no excuses for being late!

STAYING FIT AND HEALTHY

It is also important to take good care of yourself. Eat well and exercise. It can be very easy and convenient to settle into a diet of fast food and snack food when on tour. Make the effort to eat nutritious food and get some exercise. You spend a lot of time on tour in your car, on public transport, and in the pit, so make the effort to walk as much as possible and make the use of a local gym.

Tip

Most theatres will have a deal with a local gym where you can pay a daily or a weekly fee to use the facilities. Your company manager will often include such information if they send out a weekly information email, or the theatre will have it posted on the staff notice board in the theatre. If in doubt, ask the stage door staff at the theatre.

There are now gyms available in most city centres that allow you to pay for just a day or a week pass without becoming a member. In the UK the most common ones are The Gym and Pure Gym, but there are many others. Use the Internet to find out what is available in each city before travelling there. You can also consider taking a bike with you to use on tour, or you can just get out and run around the city for exercise. A good way to explore a city is to walk around for a few hours and get some exercise at the same time.

TOURING IN THE UNITED STATES

I must say that I have not personally toured with a musical in the United States, so I can't give as much detailed insight into the lifestyle as I can from my experience in the UK. I do, however, believe that much of the information in this chapter is universal and can be adapted to wherever you are in the world.

There are an average of 150 full-time AFM musicians touring throughout the United States and Canada, in over twenty musicals. Touring shows not only employ musicians that travel with the show but also provide employment to hundreds of local musicians. Most shows travel with just a small core group of musicians and then use local musicians in each town to cover the rest of the instruments needed for the show. As touched on before, the reason for this is that the United States and Canada are split into locals for each state or region, and musicians are not allowed to perform outside the local that they are registered in unless they have negotiated a prior agreement. Fines are imposed on members if the rules are broken. Every theatre will have a minimum number of musicians that need to be employed for each production (like on Broadway), and each town or local will usually have its own contractor who hires in the local musicians for the local theatres. Prior to the tour starting, an agreement will be made by the tour organisers with each local about the number of touring musicians allowed on a specific production performing.

It is common that key members of the show, like the conductor and possibly some rhythm section players, will be allowed to perform in every local, but this will have to be pre-agreed. This arrangement has been put into place by the AFM to protect jobs of musicians around the country so that not just musicians from the major cities like New York get all the work when a show is touring the country. Some shows are exempt from using local musicians if the musicians are integral to the look and the sound of the show and cannot therefore be covered by anyone else. Local musicians who are employed on touring shows will be informed of the orchestration for each show coming into town in advance by the AFM or the TMA.

What also makes touring in the United States very different from the UK is the size of the country. In the UK the comparatively small size of the country allows musicians to get between venues with relative ease. When travelling, getting between even the most distant cities can be done in a day or less. In the States it can take numerous days to drive between venues, and popping home on your day off can be an impossible task. Touring musicians in the States can spend months away from home, and many even tour their entire family with them. Because of the distances, subbing is often not permitted, or it is insisted that it can only be allowed when the tour is in a bigger city where a good substitute is easier to find. The producer must provide accommodation to musicians if they have to stay more than fifty miles from their home address and also provide per diems similar to when working abroad for UK musicians. Some musicians will choose to drive between venues, while others will choose to fly. Some shows will also have touring coaches that will take cast, crew, and musicians between cites. The travelling method used will be determined by the type of show and the touring schedule.

UK musicians cannot perform in any show in the United States on Broadway or touring unless they either have a US-approved work permit or some sort of an agreement has been made with the US government. These rules are very strict and are taken very seriously. Don't be tempted to try to work in the United States as a musician without the proper approval, since the consequences can be severe. The same goes for US musicians working in the UK. You will need to have a UK work permit to work as a musician in the UK.

12

How a Show Is Put Together

This chapter gives you a general idea of how a show is put together up to the stage where you would join the production as a musician. A lot goes on before the first band call, and a vast amount of money will have been spent even before the show opens. In fact, the setting up of a show is the most expensive time for the producers, way before any tickets are sold and any money comes in. It can take a show many months to recoup the money spent on the getting the show up and running. The audience expects a show that is well put together, with a good-looking set and great sound and choreography, so the budget for getting a show up and running can often run into the millions of pounds or dollars. As musicians, we are often totally oblivious to all this happening, but I think it is a good idea to have some understanding of how the show you are working on came to be and all the elements that make it what it is.

There are just so many factors when it comes to putting a show together that I won't be able to talk about all of them. I will run through some of the most crucial elements to give a general idea. The way things are put together will of course vary from show to show, but the basic process will stay roughly the same.

The first stage is that there is an idea for a new show, or to put on an already established show. Here the early process will be slightly different, since with a brand-new musical there will be a process of turning a raw idea into a working show, and this can take a long time, with many rewrites and changes along the way. The show will then go into a workshop phase, where things are tried and tested until it's a workable show. If a producer is not already involved, they will now be brought in to finance getting the show into a theatre. If an already established show is being remounted, a producer will usually have to buy the rights to that show so that they can legally perform in whichever territory they gained the rights. There will often be limitation with the rights, which includes where the show can be performed and for how long.

The producers will now hire a creative team to handle the setting up of the show. This will include a director, a musical supervisor, a production manager, a choreographer, a sound designer, a lighting designer, a costume designer, and a set designer. If a show is being purchased with set and costumes from a previous production, a set designer and a costume designer will possibly not be needed. An established producer will have creatives that they have worked with before, or even have people directly employed by them.

Before anything else goes ahead, a theatre will have to be secured for the duration that the show is running, or in the case of a tour, all the theatres around the country will need to be secured so that there are minimal gaps in the touring schedule, which can last anything from a few months to a number of years, depending on how the show is expected to sell. A promotional agency will also have been appointed, and they will be busy getting promotional material for the show ready, and a promotional schedule will be planned to give the show the maximum publicity in preparation for the opening. On a touring production, the process is more complicated because of the many different theatres at which the show will need to perform. A deal needs to be negotiated with every theatre on the circuit about the price of tickets and how the profits are split. Furthermore, every theatre needs to be checked to see if the set, lights, and sound equipment fit in. A production manager will usually be in charge of this, and they will need to check every venue on the tour to make sure that it is suitable for the show. Also, a haulage company will be hired to move the show from theatre to theatre. With the show moving frequently between theatres, the get-ins and get-outs for each theatre need to be planned in advance. It is common to hire in an extra team of people purely for the get-ins and get-outs of shows to speed up the process. They will often work through the night to get all the set and equipment into the trucks and then travel to the next venue, and then put it all back into the next theatre. There are many big production companies that will take on the role of financing musicals all over the world, as well as the smaller producers doing the lower-budget shows. Some will only do shows in particular cities, while others will do big tours.

The Show Musician

A casting agent will now be appointed to start finding the appropriate performers for the production, as well as a fixer/musical contractor to start putting the band together, choosing the most appropriate available musicians for the show. Sometimes the cast is chosen through an open audition, where pretty much anyone can come to audition for a part in the show, but more often people are picked by the casting agent through their personal agents, and then through the audition process the numbers are narrowed down until the appropriate people are found. The choreographer makes sure that they are capable of the dancing needed for the show, the director makes sure that they can act well enough, and the musical supervisor and MD check whether they are vocally strong enough to perform the show eight times a week and have the correct range for their parts in the show. This process can often take weeks or months and starts well before the show is due to start.

Next, the cast rehearsals start. A space is hired and a rehearsal process of four to eight weeks starts. All the creative team will be involved, including the MD and assistant MD, to get the performers ready for the show opening. On some shows the drummer, and possibly the bass player, will join the rehearsals for the last week or two to give the choreographer more support in the dance calls. Occasionally the whole band will be used, but this is rare because of the cost implications. Sometimes a special rehearsal drummer will be hired in for the rehearsals, but he or she will not do the show when up and running. This will be done if the drummer booked for the show is not available or does not live locally to the rehearsal studio. During the rehearsals the cast will also be

How a Show is Put Together

fitted for costumes and wigs, and different members of the creative team will be making changes and improvements to make sure that everything is ready in time for the move to the theatre.

If it's a new show, or a show that is undergoing a lot of musical changes, the band will sometimes be called for a rehearsal over the space of a few days. However, in most cases the band will only start a week or two before the show opening, and this will usually happen in the theatre where the first performance of the show will take place. All the different departments will at this stage be busy in the theatre getting everything ready. The stage scenery will be in the process of being assembled, and the lights being put up, as well as the sound system. The costumes are being fitted again and last-minute alterations are done.

After a Sitzprobe (see Chapter 8) is done with the band and cast, the band is moved to the pit to do a sound check. Now technical rehearsals start, where all the different parts of the show are tested and things are tweaked so that everything runs smoothly. The show is run in stages, and each scene is blocked so that it looks as good as possible. Technical rehearsals can run for many days or even weeks, depending on how complex the show is. Everything has to work and run smoothly before the first performance so that there are no show stops, and for everyone's safety on stage.

After the technical rehearsals are done, you move straight into dress rehearsal, where the show is run in its entirety with the cast in their costumes. The band will now be called in. Numerous dress rehearsals are done, and then the show goes into previews. A few preview shows are performed before the anticipated press night happens, where the theatre critics attend to review the show. This is of course a crucial time for the show, since bad reviews can seriously harm a show's success.

So there you have it. A quick run-through of the process a show goes through. This is of course simplified, and there are many people involved in this huge process that has to be organised to perfection, with both complex finance budgets and time restrictions.

13

Being Self-Employed

Being a freelance musician also means for the most part that we are also self-employed. This means that you are totally responsible for organising your own time, travel, accommodation, and finances, including taxes. We've already looked at travel and accommodation in the previous chapter, so let's have a look at some of the other elements.

TIME MANAGEMENT

You need to know where you need to be and when. This seems obvious, but you'd amazed how many musicians don't use a robust diary system. In the time of smartphones, there is really no excuse not to be organised.

Keep a well-organised diary. I would recommend using an electronic diary that automatically syncs and backs up to an online location. Some say "What's wrong with the good old traditional paper diary?" Well, nothing as long as you remember to bring it with you and you don't lose it. The advantages of having an electronic diary are manifold.

1) It is always backed up. If you happen to lose or forget your diary in one form (say your smartphone), you can always access it from another device or computer.

2) You can set reminders. This can be invaluable if you have many gigs with different bands, in different locations. It is easy to forget that Sunday lunchtime gig you were booked for months ago, when you normally have Sundays off. Many electronic calendars are now so sophisticated that they will even remind you to leave earlier because of traffic or public transport conditions.

3) If you own a smartphone, like most people today, it is always with you, and you are a lot less likely to forget that than a paper diary.

Just remember to write all those appointments in the diary as soon as they are booked, and make any amendments immediately before you forget. You don't want to be getting that phone call ten minutes before the gig starts, and you're at home with a glass of red wine thinking you have the night off because you forgot to put the gig in the diary. Sounds ridiculous? Believe me, it does happen. Get into the habit of keeping an organised diary now, if you're not doing it already. It will pay off.

Tip

Have your phone with you at all times. You don't want to miss a phone call — it could be that important gig and your big break. When musicians are looking for covers last-minute, they will often have a list of people to ring, and if you don't answer they will move to the next person on the list. If they answer and accept the gig, you will just have missed out, all because you left your phone upstairs on silent.

TAX AND MONEY MANAGEMENT

This has to be the dullest aspect of being a self-employed musician but is also one of the most important and is the one thing that many musicians overlook or neglect.

I am only personally experienced in tax matters in the UK, so I cannot give you specific tax advice on tax laws and regulations anywhere else in the world, since they vary greatly. At the end of this chapter, I give you some information on some of the differences in terminology between the UK and the US, but you will need to check any tax laws and regulations in your area, and I cannot take any responsibility for tax matters, whether it's in the UK or anywhere else in the world. Tax laws change often, so you will need to seek professional advice or look on the official government websites for information (see links at the end of this chapter). I do hope, however, that this chapter will give you some insight into how you need to organise your finances to make any tax-related matters easier to deal with and possibly demystify some of the aspects of this rather dull but necessary topic.

When you become self-employed, you automatically become responsible for paying your own taxes. If you are used to working in a nine-to-five job or where you are paid monthly by PAYE (pay as you earn), you may not have had to worry about this before, at least if you live in the UK.

> **Note**
>
> In the United States and Canada, the system is a little different to the UK, with your employer withholding some of your income as an estimate of your tax liability. You then need to fill in an Income Tax Return, which takes into account any other liabilities or extra income you may have had.

If working as PAYE in the UK, any tax and other deductions like pension and National Insurance is taken off your salary before it's deposited into your bank account. What's left you can spend as you wish, and there are no more taxes to pay, as long as you don't have any other income to declare. As a self-employed person, you have to make sure you put money aside for both tax and national insurance. You need to be a lot more organised with your money and keep a close eye on all your income and outgoings. This can be rather dull and tedious, but there is a plus side to this that a regular nine-to-five person doesn't have, and that is non-taxable expenses.

EXPENSES

This is one of the major perks of being self-employed. In basic terms, any expenses that are directly related to running

Being Self-Employed

your business as a musician you can claim off your Annual Gross Pay (your total income for the year). This will then give you your annual Net Pay (what is left after reductions), and this is what your tax liability gets calculated on. What you can claim as an expense can be something of a grey area, and the Inland Revenue (the UK tax authority) are constantly changing the rules on what is acceptable expense and what isn't.

Note

If you work in the West End, or in fact anywhere you will be staying in the same place of work for a long period of time, the rules change for expenses. You will no longer be able to claim the same expenses as when on tour. You are now classed as being in a permanent place of work, and you will no longer be able to claim expenses like subsistence and travel. If you still do other regular freelance work where you are in different places of work, that can still be claimed as an expense and might affect your status in your 'permanent place of work.' The IR refers to a place of work becoming permanent after twenty-four months, but speak to your accountant about this issue.

Your accountant should be knowledgeable about acceptable expenses, and you can find further information on your tax authority's website. Below I have listed what can generally be considered acceptable expenses for a musician. The categories mostly reflect the Inland Revenue in the UK, as seen in the self-assessment section of their website.

Travel Costs

Car fuel expenses, trains, and taxis related to getting to and from gigs and rehearsals. Any other car-related expenses, toll charges, servicing, repairs and maintenance, etc. Any non-work-related use of a vehicle will have to be calculated and cannot be claimed.

Accommodation

Any digs, hotels, and other charges related to accommodation while touring, or which are directly linked with your job as a musician.

Subsistence

This can be a bit of a grey area with the taxman, but basically includes any expenses in relation to eating and drinking (not alcohol) while on tour. Because of the hours that musicians work, you could potentially include meals out before a gig, even if you are commuting from your home, since we normally need to be in or near the venue during normal evening meal hours and can therefore not cook at home, but you will need to use your discretion on this.

Note

Accommodation and subsistence will often be classed as part of the Travel Expenses category for the IR.

Clothing

Any clothes and shoes bought to wear specifically for work. These should not be used for any other purpose.

Staff Costs

If you pay any staff in relation to your business, this includes any payment to a dep/sub.

Equipment

Any equipment bought needed for your business as a musician. Also, any repairs and maintenance costs related to your instrument and other equipment you use. The purchase of a car or van can also be claimed, but the rules vary depending on the value and type of vehicle. This can also be classed as a Capital Allowance. The IR classifies capital allowance as anything you buy to keep in your business. For example, equipment, machinery, and vehicles.

Office Expenses

Any expenses related to running an office.

Your mobile phone bill. Normally a percentage is claimed, personal against business expenses.

Stationery and printing and postage. For example, printing of any work promotion material, business cards, etc.

Financial Costs

Insurance you need like instrument insurance and possibly travel insurance.

Any bank charges and finance charges. For example, charges related to a business account and interest on any business-related loans.

Business Premises

If you need to hire storage or a practise room, or if you rent an office space. You can sometimes claim a percentage of the expense of using a room in your house as an office or a practise room.

Advertising and Media

Cost of running a website and any other work-related advertising.

Media. Any audio or video bought in relation to work. Research to learn a new show or to expand your music knowledge on your instrument.

Health and Fitness

If you need to stay fit, whether it's going to the gym or seeing a physiotherapist, as long as you show that it's needed because of playing an instrument. You need to have a certain amount of fitness to sustain long periods of holding a heavy instrument and have the stamina to play eight shows a week for long periods of time. Also, injuries can happen. Therefore, in some instances you can claim a percentage of your health and fitness expenses.

Do you really need to know any of this stuff? Can't you just get an accountant to sort it all out for you?' The answer is yes, you can, but it can be helpful to know some of the details about what you can and cannot claim. This can help you keep your accounts in order, which can potentially lower your accountancy bill and possibly your tax bill. If you want further explanation on this topic, go to the government website. See links at the end of the chapter.

DO I NEED AN ACCOUNTANT?

Legally you do not need an accountant, and you can do your accounts yourself and just fill in your self-assessment tax return online. However, you will need to read up on a lot of tax-related jargon so that you know how to fill in your tax return correctly, although the online Inland Revenue system is relatively straightforward.

Using an accountant is a good idea if you have no idea how the tax self-assessment system works, since an accountant can give you good advice and keeps up with any changes in the law. They can also suggest minimising your tax liability through ways that you would possibly never have thought of, especially if your business as a musician is varied and incorporates different elements of playing, teaching, studio work, composing, etc. If your business is straightforward, there is no reason why you couldn't do your own accounts; just make sure that you read up on the latest tax legislation with regards to self-employment. If you decide to form a limited company or go VAT (value added tax) registered, I would recommend having an accountant, since your accounts will be much more complicated.

Choosing an Accountant

The life of a working musician can be very different to many other professions, so make sure that any accountant you use is familiar with the theatre side of things and that they have an understanding of the lifestyle that a musician lives, especially when on tour, and what can be claimed as an expense. Ask them questions like: 'Have you represented others in the entertainment industry?' 'Are you aware of different aspects of the touring musician's expenses?' Get a personal recommendation if you can, and always get a price estimate before you sign up. Your accountant does not necessarily need to be local to you. Most things can be done electronically now, or by post, so get a cheaper service even if it's not in your local area.

Whether or not you use an accountant, you will need to keep receipts for anything that you buy that you intend on claiming back on the business. Also, make sure that all invoicing is in order. If you pay for everything on debit or credit card, the record of it leaving your account on your bank statement is usually enough, but I would still keep receipts if you can, just in case.

Never withhold any income from your accounts. If you do get investigated by the tax authorities and they find discrepancies and you have not been declaring parts of your income, it can be classed as fraud. My advice is to always do your accounts as honestly as possible, whether you use an accountant or not.

What Can I Expect to Pay for an Accountant?

This can vary greatly depending on whether you're a sole trader or a limited company, and if you're VAT-registered. It also depends on how you present your accounts to your accountant. The more work they have to do, the more they will charge. In the UK you can expect to pay in the region of £150–£500 as a sole trader, with reasonably organised accounts, £500–£1000+ for a limited company, and a little extra if you're VAT-registered. Prices can vary greatly between areas and firms, so shop around.

ORGANISING YOUR ACCOUNTS

Being organised is the most sensible way to make your accountancy as easy as possible and minimising your accountancy bills. Get into a habit of sorting out your receipts and invoices on a monthly or even weekly basis. Find a system that works for you; whether it's a traditional filing system or a computer-based system is up to you. Choose what you feel the most comfortable with. Just make sure that it's simple and quick.

I prefer to use a software-based system where I download my statements from my bank into the program, and then sort them into the relevant categories from there. At the end of the tax year I just email my accountant the breakdown of income and expenses by category. There are many decent brands of personal finance software available; just make sure that they are reputable companies and have good data security in place. Most of them will offer a free trial, so use that to make sure that the service offers everything you need.

Find what works for you and even have a chat with your accountant about how they prefer to receive your accounts. Many will be happy with just a copy of your bank statements for the year and your receipts. The main object is to find a system that is quick and simple and works for you and your accountant, with minimum risk of errors.

Saving For Tax

How much tax you pay is of course totally related to your earnings and how many expenses you are able to claim. To work out your estimated tax liability, there are a few things you need to take into account. Now, this is only for sole traders, since limited companies are much more complex.

The first thing you need to be aware of is your personal allowance. This is how much you can earn before you have to pay any tax. You take your business expenses off your gross income, which gives you your net income, then take off your personal allowance, and that is the amount that your tax liability is calculated on, as well as your national insurance (see below). The percentage of tax you pay depends on the tax bracket you are in. If your net income crosses a certain threshold, your tax liability could jump considerably, so check what those thresholds are so you don't get stung. In the UK at the time of writing the higher rate of tax starts around £45,000 a year, which would be your net earnings.

Check your local tax authority website for the latest rate of tax if you want to work out your tax liability in more detail. At the time of writing, in the UK the personal allowance is £10,000, and the basic rate of tax is 20%. You will also have to pay National Insurance; see below for further information.

Be aware that you will also need to pay on account. This is especially important in your first year of trading.

Paying on account is where you pay 50% of your tax again in advance on next year's liability. In the UK tax is due before 31st of January each year. In your first year of trading you will need to pay a further 50% on top of your tax liability, and then 50% on account again in July each year. If your income stayed the same as the previous year, then this amount will remain about the same and be payable twice a year. However, if your income went up from the previous year, a balancing payment would also be due to cover the difference. Payment on account can potentially hit hard in your first year of trading as self-employed, but it then becomes a rolling payment, and your tax liability should become more consistent in the following years. There can be a lot to pay in your first year as self-employed, so make sure that you put that money aside throughout the year in preparation. Of course, check tax liabilities and other taxes payable in your country or state to get a more accurate idea of tax due.

UK NATIONAL INSURANCE

National Insurance in the UK is a system of contributions paid towards the cost of certain state benefits, including the state pension. If you are an employee, are over sixteen, and earn more than £155 a week, you have to pay class 1 national insurance. This is calculated automatically and deducted from your salary. If you are self-employed and making a profit of more than £5,965 a year, you have to pay class 2 National Insurance at £2.80 a week. You will also have to pay class 4 National Insurance at 9% of profits above £8,060. All figures are correct as of time of writing.

Registering as Self-Employed

In the UK you have register as self-employed within a certain time of starting to be paid for self-employed work. The process is pretty easy these days and can be done online. You go to the Inland Revenue website and register as a self-employed. You will then be sent a letter within a few days with your online log-in username and password. If you have an accountant, they can do this for you if you like and will then act as your representative to the Inland Revenue.

The tax year in the UK runs from the 6th of April to the 5th of April. Basically, you need to keep any receipts from the 6th of April each year to the 5th of April the following year, inclusive. However, whatever date you register your business will become your business year. So if you start being self-employed on the 15th of September, your tax year essentially runs from the 16th of September to the 15th of September the following year, inclusive. You still need to submit your tax return at the same time, before the 31st of January each year. If it's late, you will incur a fine.

In the US the tax year runs from the 1st of January to the 31st of December each year.

When you register for self-employment, you can register as a sole trader, which is the most basic and easiest to deal with in tax terms, or you can register as a limited company. Let's have a look at these in more detail.

Sole Trader

You are the only person involved in the business and have full accountability. You have to submit a tax return once a year, and you can claim business expenses off your total income. You will need to pay national insurance class 2 and class 4. This is calculated on your net income and is paid as part of your self-assessment.

LIMITED COMPANY

Being registered as a limited company is more complex than being a sole trader but can have its benefits if done properly. I would recommend registering your limited company through your accountant and have them deal with your accounts. You will need a business account with a bank, and you will need to register your company with Companies House in the UK. Go to gov.uk for more info. Look carefully at whether it's worth going from sole trader to a limited company. A limited company has many more expenses than a sole trader, bigger accountancy bills, business account charges, etc.

For the long-running shows in the UK, a sole trader will usually be put on the payroll for the show and gets a pay slip every week. They will not have to invoice the company, and the money will be paid directly into their bank account every week, usually on a Friday. As a limited company, you will need to invoice your employer for every show you do. This can be on a weekly basis or for individual gigs, depending on the arrangement. The money will still go into your account automatically each week, but you will have to have invoiced for that to happen. For one-off gigs it is usual that both sole traders and limited companies will need to invoice for payment. Your accountant will be able to advise you on how best to manage your accounts and if being a limited company is worth your while.

VAT

VAT stands for value added tax and is a tax added to most retail products and services in the UK (20% at time of writing). It is payable to the government. The benefit of being VAT-registered in the UK is that you can invoice your employer an extra 20% on top of your regular salary. Don't be fooled, though, since this is not really your money. You will have to pay back most, if not all of that extra 20% back to the government. Another big advantage of being VAT-registered is that you can purchase equipment from other companies that are VAT-registered (which includes most retail companies), and not pay VAT on those purchases, so basically you get a 20% discount off the products you buy. However, the government will also assume that 20% off every invoice you submit for work done has VAT added, which then has to be paid back to the government, at least in part. You will also need to do your accounts more frequently, with your VAT returns submitted every three months.

There are too many rules in regards to VAT to go into here in detail, so I would advise you to talk to your accountant if you are thinking about going VAT-registered. If your total gross income exceeds £83,000 (correct at the time of writing), you will have to go VAT-registered whether you want to or not, and you will from then on need to charge VAT on all your business transactions and keep accounts for all the VAT charged and paid. The VAT threshold usually increases on a yearly basis, so check with your accountant or the IR for the current figure.

The US does not have a VAT system like the UK; instead, a state sales tax is charged, which varies between states. Again, check with your accountant about the best way to manage your tax affairs in your region.

ACCOUNTING SOFTWARE

There is an ever-increasing choice of great financial software on the market, and many are now offering services that are cloud (online)-based. These services can potentially save you time and effort when it comes to your finances and your tax, but you will have to explore which one suits you best and will provide the most benefit compared to cost. If you have an accountant, check with them what would be the best option to save them time and what the best way is to streamline the process of getting your accounts in. If they don't charge you any more for just having your bank statements for the year, maybe that's the way to go, but if you can streamline the process further and cut costs, it might be worth exploring some software tools to help.

Most of these services or software offer a trial period so you can always explore what they offer in more detail. Just be careful with online services that claim they are free. How they normally finance their operation is to sell your financial information to third-party companies that will then target product offers to you, like loans. Just make sure that you read the T&C's carefully before signing up.

The most important features you need to have are:

- A way to import your bank statements easily and reliably, either using a qif export format from your online banking, which you then import into the accounting software, or preferably an automated bank transaction method.

- You need to be able to categorise your transactions into the relevant expense category in an easy and quick way. For example, car expenses, accommodation expenses, etc.

- You need to be able to produce a report for your tax year that has an itemised record of all your income and expenses for all your different categories.

- An invoicing feature can also be helpful, although you can do that on a word processor or using another dedicated service.

US Variations

Sole trader is referred to as a sole proprietor.

Limited company is referred to as a corporation. A limited liability company, LLC, can also be considered, but the rules that govern LLC's are state-dependent.

Being Self-Employed

USEFUL TAX RESOURCES

In the UK: The Inland Revenue www.gov.uk

In the US: The IRS www.irs.gov

14

Other Useful Information

Here you can find some information and links to theatre and other music related resources that might be useful.

MUSICIANS' UNION IN THE UK (MU)

Head Office

60-62 Clapham Road,

London

SW9 0JJ

Tel: 02075825566

Website

www.musiciansunion.org.uk

www.facebook.com/Musicians.Union

Other Useful Information

AMERICAN FEDERATION OF MUSICIANS (AFM)

New York Headquarters

1501 Broadway

Suite 600

New York, NY 10036

Phone: (212) 869-1330

Legislative Office

5335 Wisconsin Ave. NW

Suite 440

Washington, DC 20015

Phone: (202) 274-4756

Canadian Office

150 Ferrand Drive

Suite #202

Toronto, Ontario M3C 3E5

Phone: (416) 391-5161

West Coast Office

817 Vine St.

Hollywood, CA 90038

Phone: (323) 461-5401

Website

www.afm.org

www.facebook.com/afm.org

OTHER USEFUL WEBSITES AND RESOURCES

The Stage (UK): www.thestage.co.uk

Broadway Shows: www.broadway.com

Playbill (US): www.playbill.com

Tax-related resources

UK: The Inland Revenue: www.gov.uk/government/organisations/hm-revenue-customs

US: Internal Revenue Service: www.irs.gov/Businesses/Small-Businesses-&-Self-Employed

USA Government Information: www.usa.gov/start-business

Other

The Show Musician Website: www.showmusician.com

Other Useful Information

ESSENTIAL LISTENING

As mentioned before, it's important to listen to and have an understanding of most styles of music when working on shows and if you intend to work as professional musician. Consider listening and exploring music as part of your practise regime.

In musicals, especially, there is so much overlap and use of different styles and genres of music, so the more styles you can comfortably play, as well as having an understanding of the crucial elements of each style, the more authentic and ultimately better your playing will sound. Try to listen to and play as many styles of music as you can, and don't just narrow your studies to show music or the style of music that you like the most. Broaden those horizons and expand your knowledge.

Do your own research, sign up with an online music streaming service like Apple Music, Spotify, Google Play, or Amazon Prime Music and start exploring. A good starting point is to find a compilation album from each decade, starting from the 1920s and 1930s, and check out the most popular music of that time and then expand from there. Check out the artists on these compilation albums and then find more music by those artists.

If you are booked to play a show which is set in the 1980s, check out the music from that period and figure out, depending on your instrument, what the guitar sounds were like, what guitars were being used, what drums were being used, how were they tuned, and what the production was like, etc. Any new show you take on, try to find any previous versions of the show and listen to those recordings. If the show is a musical based on other well-known music or a movie, make sure that you really study the original recordings. Shows like *Mamma Mia, Dirty Dancing, We Will Rock You, Grease,* and many more fall into this category.

Creating a comprehensive listening guide is a difficult task. There are so many different artists that are relevant, and it's hard to prioritise who is more influential or more important. I believe that it's best to just get out there and start exploring using my suggestions above as a starting point. See what you find by searching these categories and expand from there. Enjoy!

- Musicals
- Big Band
- Jazz
- Rock'n'Roll
- Motown
- Country
- Funk
- Hip Hop
- Rock
- '20s Music
- '30s Music etc., by decade

Closing

Thank you for purchasing and reading my book. I hope that this book has given you some valuable information and insight into the world of the show musician and can help you both in finding work and sustaining a long and successful career in music. Working as a musician in musical theatre can be an extremely fun and rewarding job, and I wish you all the best on your journey.

If you can find the time to leave a review of the book on Amazon, or wherever you purchased it, that would be most appreciated. Also, please share with your friends and colleagues if you found this book helpful, and if you have any stories or tips to share for other show musicians, please go to showmusician.com and leave a comment. Hopefully, as a community of musicians we can help to keep the work of show musicians around the world flourishing for many years to come and help to keep the industry fair and professional for all who work in it. It is my hope that we can educate the public at large about the immense skills that musicians have that work in musical theatre, and the integral part we play in the production of a musical so that shows will never do away with live music in the orchestral pits around the world.

Appendix

Glossary of Terms Used in Theatre

Here are some terms that are used throughout this book, some of which might be unfamiliar to you. Some are specific to shows and theatre work, and some may vary between countries and regions. These are some of the most common terms used that I am aware of.

AFM: American Federation of Musicians — The American Musicians Union.

ASM: Assistant stage manager

Aviom: The digital mixer used for monitoring for musicians.

Backstage: The area behind the stage. Where dressing rooms are for cast, and other areas not open to the public.

Blacks: The black clothes that musicians and technical teams need to wear in the pit and on stage. They are black so that they don't stand out and disrupt the look of the show.

Balanced Connection: A way to connect sound equipment using balanced cables, which reduces noise picked up by the cables, especially on long cable runs.

Blocking: A process that is usually done by the choreographer of a show. A term used for spacing out the performers on the stage so that the show looks symmetrical

Appendix

from the audience, and so that the space on the stage is used to its full potential.

Bylaws: The rules and regulations enacted by an association or a corporation to provide a framework for its operation and management. The AFM and the TMA each have their own bylaws.

Cans: Headphones that cover the ears.

Chaperon: A person that looks after any underage performers on a show.

ClearSonic: Refers to acoustic screening. ClearSonic is a brand name for acoustic screening. Can be clear, see-through or solid soft panels. Commonly used around drum kits and other acoustic instruments to minimise sound spillage into the auditorium, or into microphones for other instruments nearby.

CM: Company manager

Company Office: Where the company manager sets up an office in the theatre backstage.

DI: Direct inject or direct input. Any sound equipment that is connected directly into the sound desk and PA and does not use an amplifier.

DI Box: Used to directly connect instruments to the sound desk. Converts an unbalanced connection to a balanced one.

Digs: A term used in the industry for accommodation. Includes hotels, bed & breakfasts, or indeed anywhere you might stay while working away from home.

DSM: Deputy stage manager

Entr'acte: The opening music to Act 2 of a show. Means 'Between the Acts.'

EPK: Electronic press kit. A combination of promotional material used to advertise a theatre production in the media, including TV and radio.

Equity: A trade union representing professional performers and creative practitioners in the UK. Called the Actors' Equity in the US.

Fixer: The person who is contracted by the producers to 'fix' the band for the show. He or she will contact each musician and put together a suitable group of musicians for the production. Also a point of contact for members of the band.

Flying: A term used for scenery or anything that is flown in from above of the stage. Usually controlled by a flyman.

Front of House: The area where the general public resides. The auditorium, bars, and box office, etc.

Gig: A term used for a musical engagement. Can be paid or unpaid.

Groove: A general music term to describe how a piece of music feels. Other terms are use to describe the same

Appendix

thing in different styles of music, 'swing' in jazz music, 'the pocket' in funk, etc. It essentially means that the music feels good and that the musicians playing are totally in sync with each other.

In-ears: Headphones that go inside the ear canal.

Local 802: The Broadway Local. The AFM is split into numerous local regions across North America. Local 802 refers to New York City and Broadway. Local 6 is the San Francisco local, for example.

LX: Lighting and special effects. The technical team that handles lights and other special effects for the show.

MD: Musical director

Musical Contractor: Same as a fixer but a title used in the US.

Overture: The opening music to a show. Usually contains a mixture of the songs in the show.

PA System: Public address system. An electronic sound amplification and distribution system.

Pamphlet B: The agreement used by the AFM for touring musicians in the US and Canada.

PAT Test: Portable Appliance Test is the term used to describe the examination of electrical appliances and equipment to ensure they are safe to use. Is compulsory in some circumstances in theatres.

Physical Warmup: A warmup the dance captain conducts before the show to get the cast warmed physically for the show. Normally happens just before vocal warmup and is particularly important on dance-heavy shows.

Post-fade: Sound that does get affected by the sound operator changing the volume on the mixing console.

Pre-fade: Sound that does not get affected by the sound operator moving the faders on the mixing console. For instance, if your monitor mix is pre-fade, then the volume of your mix should not change if even if the volume is turned up in the front-of-house PA system.

QLab: A piece of music software used to run tracks and clicks on shows.

Safety curtain: The curtain that comes down at the front of the stage before the show and in the interval. It's a fire curtain to contain fire that could potentially start backstage during a show. It is a legal requirement for theatres to have it down when the performance is not in action.

Show Report: A report that is created at the end of each and every performance listing any issues that may have occurred during the performance. This report then is sent off to all the show's creatives at the end of each day. This is done to keep a track of and to document recurring issues in a show.

Sitting In: A UK term for watching a musician playing the show.

Sitzprobe: The first performance of the show with the vocals in a rehearsal situation.

SM: Stage manager

Appendix

Stage right/left: A reference to each side of the stage when looking from the stage into the auditorium.

Stick: The baton used by the musical director to conduct the band.

Swing: A performer who covers numerous parts in the show in case of emergency. They will learn specific parts in the show and will have to cover those, often at a moment's notice.

The Book: Refers to the written music in a show. Mainly a US term. Can also be called the Pad or The Music. 'Watching the book' is the same as 'sitting in' in the UK.

The Pad: A term used for the written music in a show. Same as the book in the US.

TMA: Theatre Musician Association. A non-profit organisation in the US that represents all theatre musicians. TMA was also a term for the touring agreement for musicians in the UK and stood for Theatre Management Association. It has now been renamed UKT — UK Theatre.

UKT: The current agreement for UK touring theatre musicians.

Underscore: A piece of music that is played underneath a scene in the show where the vocals need to be heard. Usually played very quietly.

Understudy: A performer who covers a specific part in the show but only goes onstage to perform on occasion, or as an emergency if the main performer can't because of injury, illness, or holiday.

Vocal Warmup: A warmup conducted by the MD or assistant MD to get the cast warmed up vocally before the show. Usually done about an hour before the show starts on stage.

Watching the Book: The US term for sitting in. Watching a musician play the show.

Wedge: A stage monitor speaker, which gets its name from its wedge shape.

The Wings: The sides of the stage that are hidden from view of the audience. Used to store pieces of set and where the cast waits to come onstage.

Made in the USA
Middletown, DE
19 December 2019